Two Falls, Two Submissions or a Knockout

Two Falls, Two Submissions or a Knockout

Al Marquette

ATHENA PRESS
LONDON

TWO FALLS, TWO SUBMISSIONS, OR A KNOCKOUT
Copyright © Al Marquette 2007

All Rights Reserved

No part of this book may be reproduced in any form
by photocopying or by any electronic or mechanical means,
including information storage or retrieval systems,
without permission in writing from both the copyright
owner and the publisher of this book.

ISBN 10-digit: 1 84748 150 7
ISBN 13-digit: 978 1 84748 150 4

First Published 2007 by
ATHENA PRESS
Queen's House, 2 Holly Road
Twickenham TW1 4EG
United Kingdom

Printed for Athena Press

So You Want to Be a Wrestler, My Son?

So you want to be a wrestler, lad,
I'll tell you what to do,
Get an awful lot of training,
And the best of coaching too,
Lead a life that's clean,
And you may pass the test,
But it'll take at least five years or so,
To mingle with the best.

You are going to meet lots of boys,
Who are maybe just as hot,
You'll have to take more beatings,
But don't let it break your heart,
Just keep plugging all the time,
Never do say 'Die'!
The guys who get on top of the heap,
Are those who always try.

You will get bad ears, infections,
Torn ligaments, burns and cuts,
But just keep going right along,
And show you have the guts,
Then someday when you are thru',
And just don't give a damn,
At least in the final consensus,
They will say, 'There was a Man!'

Bob 'Rebel' Russell

Contents

Acknowledgements	ix
Foreword by Johnny Briggs	xi
Preface	xiii
The Blood Tub	15
No More Mr Nice Guy	20
The Sad Demise of the Great Mitsi Moto	26
All in the Family	35
Grand Halls, Bear Pits and Loaded Handbags	44
Heroes and Villains	48
The Meanest Gunslinger in the (North) West and Other Crowd Pullers	57
Kings, Queens and a Black Comedy	69
The (Even More) Eccentrics	79
The Masked Men	90
Wrestling for Charity	99
The Reunion	111
The Best of Times	114

Acknowledgements

In researching this book I have come into contact with many former wrestlers and promoters, and I cannot thank them enough for all the information and photographs that they have given or loaned without any reservation.

They have relived again with me the years, and I hope that they have enjoyed the memories as much as I have. Peter Fletcher, Jack Taylor, Colin Joynson, Steve Haggerty, Bert Royal, Bob Bell, Roy St Clair and Jackie Robinson have all contributed to the content and humour of this book.

Regarding the computer technology involved, with endless gratitude I thank Tony Ellis; the man is a keyboard wizard. Also for his invaluable help, my son-in-law, Andrew Greenfield, not forgetting the skill of the professional photographer, Stewart Derby.

All have contributed to the compilation of this book and I hope you will enjoy reading it.

Foreword

When Al asked me to provide words to open his book I was only too delighted to say yes for the reasons I will now recount. I met Al near enough thirty years ago at Northenden Golf Club where he was wandering around at about 6.30 a.m. He was playing golf, I was playing golf and we both nodded at each other though we'd never met and Al asked me if I was on my own. I told him I was and as he was also playing alone, we palled up and he took money off me and I've been trying to win it back ever since. They don't call Al the Silver Fox for nothing, believe me.

What did I make of this gentle-looking middle-aged man? Well, I thought he was a bandit, plain and simple. He told me what his handicap was and I thought I could have a go at him but then he explained he was an ex-wrestler – retired – so I just agreed and smiled, giving him the money before exiting stage left.

Fooling around aside, that day in the early morning mists of the golf course was the beginning of an incredible friendship that has seen us become part of each other's families, sharing happy and sad times but always enjoying being in one another's company. So why did we hit it off so well? For me, that's easy to answer. Al took me as an ordinary guy, not a television actor or famous name; to Al, I was a friend and that was it. There was no pretence of trying to be my friend because of who I was; he was just an ordinary guy, as I am, and I think that's how we've carried on through all these years, and why so many people ask, 'Is that your father?', which I think is hysterical!

I've only ever seen him annoyed once and that was when we were in Portugal with my son and this woman came up and said, 'Ooh, I know who you three are.'

'Really?' said Al. 'You know who I am?'

'Yes,' she replied. 'That's Johnny Briggs, that's his son and you're his father.'

Al said shortly after that the next man or woman to say that was going to get flattened! Fortunately, nobody else did... that day.

Al's been over to my home in America four or five times over the years and I really enjoy his company. He's a nice guy but he tends to keep me up too late drinking red wine. In short, eighty-one years old or not, he's a bad influence. I usually go to bed and leave him to it – some of us need our rest.

In all the years we've been friends, we've never had an argument – two life sentences worth of time. Surely that deserves some kind of medal? Nobody I've ever come across has ever told me that they didn't like Al. People just tell me what a nice guy they think he is and that's how all my close friends are because I only mix with nice people. I find that anyone I've introduced Al to has got along with him and the same applies to any one of his friends that he's introduced me to.

I feel proud and honoured that Al has asked me to write this introduction because to me, he's the father I never really had. I never knew my own dad and in a way I think Al feels I'm the son that he never had. We get on better than a father and son because we have this great bond of friendship and I'm very proud of what he's done and I'm privileged to have known him for so long.

I hope we're still friends in another thirty years. If we are, no doubt the old rascal will still be taking money off me on the golf courses around the world.

I'd consider it money well spent.

Johnny Briggs,
Manchester 2004

Preface

On Wednesday, 9 November 1955, a sports commentator and disc jockey introduced a new programme to television: *Professional Wrestling* from ringside at the West Ham Baths in London.

The name of the commentator was Kent Walton, and, after about 5,000-or-so bouts, his name became synonymous with the sport.

Born in Cairo, Egypt in 1919 of English parents, he served with the Canadian Air Force during the war and afterwards continued his acting career both on stage and in many TV appearances. He also compèred many light entertainment shows including *Answers Please* and *Cool for Cats*.

It was a telephone call from the Head of Sport for Associated Rediffusion, Ken Johnstone, that changed his life. He rang Kent and asked him what he knew about wrestling.

'Nothing,' he replied.

'Then find out,' said Johnstone. 'You need to be an expert by next Wednesday. You're commentating at the West Ham Baths.'

Kent contacted Johnny Dale of Dale-Martins Promotions in London, who whisked him around the country to watch wrestlers in action. He also introduced him to Mike Marino, one of the top heavyweights, who took him into the ring and gave him a practical demonstration of the various holds and throws.

The bouts were always filmed on Wednesday evenings, the first two being transmitted at 11 p.m. the same evening, but because of the lateness of the hour, did not appear to attract the same viewing audience as the Saturday programme.

The reaction to wrestling from the viewing public was sensational. At 4 p.m. to 5 p.m. every Saturday afternoon grandmothers and grandfathers, mums and dads and children, would be glued to their television sets cheering their heroes and booing the villains.

Mick McManus, Jackie Pallo, Steve Logan, George Kidd, Les Kellet, and of course the great tag teams, the Royal Brothers,

Colin Joynson and Steve Haggerty, Roy and Tony St Clair and many others would become household names along with Big Daddy and Giant Haystacks. Cauliflower ears, broken noses and bruises were occupational hazards for these very skilful and entertaining athletes, affectionately known as the 'grunt and groaners'.

Kent received thousands of letters during the twenty-five years he was commentating, mostly enquiring about the cuts and bruises he had sustained when men weighing 15 st. or more were hurled over the top rope, often deliberately, and landed on him. There were also questions asking him how Jackie Pallo, Steve Logan, Mick McManus and all the other hard cases, reacted to some of his comments on the liberties they took with their opponents and referees.

Such was his brilliance as a commentator that he could influence the viewing audience to a fanatical like or dislike of individual wrestlers.

It was a great era that I feel will never be repeated. The good times, the funny and sad times, all evoke wonderful memories.

These are the wrestling legends of which this book is about.

The Blood Tub

'I know you all and I'll catch you, one at a time!'

I was born in 1923, the youngest of a family of four siblings, comprising two elder brothers and a sister. It was just after the First World War and, in comparison with many at that time, I suppose we could have been called well off.

My father was a master painter and decorator and had his own business, so when I say 'well off', I didn't mean wealthy by any means. All the ladders, paint pots and paraphernalia needed had to be loaded on to, and then transported by handcart, sometimes a distance covering three miles, and often uphill.

My father was a tall man, as indeed are my two brothers and I, quietly spoken, and mildly mannered. He proudly sported a fine bushy moustache and took great pride in his appearance, from the top of his head of iron-grey hair to the highly polished boots on his feet.

His generous nature disguised his Achilles Heel; boy, did he love to gamble.

He was a member of a group of local businessmen and they would meet regularly, either in the local pub or at each other's houses. I don't know how high the stakes would reach, but when they ran out of money they would play for any personal effects: watches, rings and even the clothes that they were wearing – overcoats, scarves and gloves. When all else failed household items were staked – clocks, radios, tools – and whatever their wives' reactions were to the empty spaces that appeared in their kitchens and living rooms is best left to the imagination.

I remember one Saturday morning, when I was quite small, my mother rushing out of the house as a pony and trap appeared on our drive. It seemed that one of the group, unable to meet his gambling debt, had put up his small daughter's trap as his stake and had lost it, and my father had happened to be the winner! My mother was livid, and demanded that it was to be returned before the little girl missed it.

Another time, a few years later, just after breakfast my father said to me, 'Your first job today, son, is to empty the paint shed and pile everything up at the end of the garden and cover it all with tarpaulins.'

Seemingly, he had offered the shed the previous evening as his stake and had lost it.

It was a huge shed and clearing it out took practically the whole day – there were ladders, paste tables and dozens of cans of paint, brushes of all sizes and it was a mammoth job stacking the paint cans in their appropriate colours. Finally it was all done, but I cannot describe the kerfuffle and confusion it caused as we scrounged around under the canvas to find what we needed for the job. The recipient of our paint shed lived directly behind us, so the door on our side was locked and barred, and a new access door was fitted to the other side.

I cannot remember my mother's reaction at the time and maybe it is just as well, but a few months later my father managed to buy back the shed, as we were moving house to the other side of town. So that broke up the little gambling clique.

When I was a youngster during the thirties and early forties, Sunday afternoons were the highlight of my week. I would catch a tram from Hazel Grove, close to my home, and I would travel to Ardwick Green, via Stockport, to watch professional wrestling. I've often been asked, 'Why wrestling? Why not go to watch City or United, or Lancashire?' I can't say for sure, but the sport certainly drew me in. Perhaps because I was a bugger for fighting at school! I enjoyed the physical challenge and my schooldays maybe played a bigger part than I've ever given them credit for in the past.

Aged twelve, I was a thin, weedy kid and I didn't take kindly to anyone trying to bully me – invariably I would go in headfirst if anybody tried to push me around. I enjoyed a good ruck! My zero tolerance for school bullies came to a head one day when I was involved in an incident that would deter anyone from messing around with me again. This lad – a known bully – was waiting for me as I came out of school, Marple Willows in Stockport. Like all bullies, he had his stooges who followed him around and there were four other boys with him as I passed by. The bully grabbed me and two of the other lads grabbed my arms and held them through the railings while he began slapping me across the face with a pair of gloves. He reckoned I'd said something to him in the playground that he didn't like and I was about to pay for it

They eventually let me go on my way but this wasn't finished as far as I was concerned... far from it. About a week later, I collared the bully when he was on his own and I gave him the biggest pasting he'd ever had in his life in the schoolyard in front of all the other kids. He never did it again. I detected a kind of respect after that from my peers and perhaps the warning I had shouted to the bully's stooges convinced everyone I meant business. I pointed at the lads who'd held me against the railings and said, 'I know you all and I'll catch you, one at a time!' They never bothered me again, but the episode hadn't quite concluded. Years later, after I'd begun teaching judo at my club in Stockport, one of the lads who had been a stooge for the bully came in asking to join the club. He obviously didn't recognise me.

I asked if he'd brought any gear with him and he said he had, so I said, 'Get it on. I'll give you your first lesson.' I gave him a bruising hour or so and he never came back again.

So wrestling and physical combat certainly appealed to me and I never missed the trips to watch the men who had become my heroes. Tucked away down a cul-de-sac opposite the Manchester Hippodrome was the Ardwick Stadium, also known as 'The Blood Tub'. Comparisons could not be drawn with other big halls such as the King's Hall, Belle Vue Manchester or the Liverpool Stadium, but for me, and I expect many others, there was no place like it.

As you entered, the smell of sweat, liniment, cigarette and cigar smoke permeated the nostrils. It was wonderful excit_ng, heady stuff to a youngster. The ring canvas was permanently stained with blood, and most of the ringside seats were smashed through wrestlers being aimed over the ropes and landing on them; whatever became of the fans sitting on them defies explanation.

Advertising the bouts in the local papers or fly posting was an unnecessary exercise, since a poster pinned to the door of the stadium with the bouts of the day would attract a queue of the same regular fans, myself included, week after week.

Discussions of the merits of particular favourites would result in lively, even-tempered differences of opinion. Names debated would include Jack Pye, Francis Gregory, Jack Atherton, Vic Hesselle, Charlie Green, Man Mountain Benny, Dick the Dormouse, The Red Devil, Farmer's Boy, Bert Assirati and many more of the regular contestants who appeared there. They were all household names long before television and were big, fit and hard skilled men, and I would sit on the edge of my seat, pulling my cap to pieces in my excitement.

To the rhythm of the swaying tram on my way home I would relive every bout, feeling every forearm smash, body slam, monkey climb, suplex and arm lock, never dreaming that one day I would be climbing into the ring myself at famous halls all around the country including Belle Vue, Liverpool Stadium and the Royal Albert Hall, London, to face the sons of some of these very tough men.

They needed to be tough in those early days for, to get to the venues without today's luxury of the car, they would spend almost half of their lives on draughty, rain-soaked railway platforms; standing all, or most of the way on crowded trains and, if they were lucky enough for their bout to appear before the interval, they could catch a train back the same night. If not, it meant a local B&B or even a sleep in the station waiting room to catch the first train the following morning. This could be repeated perhaps up to three times a week.

Although I had a car in my early days, I would have to travel with a blanket over my legs and a hot water bottle on my knees since the car did not have a heater. Driving over Shap Fell on my way to Scottish venues was not a picnic; motorways were still in the future. Also in the future was the Clean Air Act and pea soup fogs and icy roads made many journeys a nightmare.

In the halls, conditions were really not much better; the dressing rooms were often cold and draughty and facilities were primitive, to say the least. A St John Ambulance man or woman on duty was a welcome sight; it meant that any injury would be treated by them instead of your doing it yourself or even taking a trip to the local hospital. They were a Godsend. Can you imagine today's American wrestling heroes in those situations?

Growing up in the 1920s and 1930s, we inhabited a different world from the one familiar to today's youngsters; discipline was more enforced, both at school and in the home. When we arrived home from school, there were jobs to be done around the home and errands to be run, but at the earliest opportunity we would be straight out of the door and into the street to play.

In the summer we played cricket on a nearby field and in the winter it was football with two coats for goalposts. We would have to be practically dragged indoors for tea and then straight out again, until we were called in for the night. Without the distraction of television, play still continued with siblings in the form of card games, ludo, snakes and ladders, etc., all serving to maintain a desire to win.

All this activity kept us very fit and, perhaps more importantly, very competitive, and upon reaching our teens we could join the local lads' club or cadet force where the emphasis was placed upon physical sports such as boxing, wrestling and judo. I also enjoyed Indian club swinging which expanded the lungs and stretched the muscles in the arms and shoulders.

The discipline paid off for me in later years during my judo training, learning to fall correctly and taking the big bumps such as body slams and suplexes. You must learn to get the feet down quickly, so preventing the base of the spine hitting the ring floor before the feet and consequently risking a spinal injury. You must also keep control when thrown over the top ropes, again by turning the body to allow the feet the first contact with the floor rather than the body.

Just as important is stamina. Any of you at some time must have fooled around with a pal or a colleague, pulling and pushing each other and gasping for breath after a couple of minutes. Wrestlers could be in the ring for forty-five minutes of virtually non-stop wrestling, being bounced around by opponents who very often could be 2 or 3 st. heavier than themselves, and believe me, that takes stamina, achieved by hours of skipping with a rope and miles of running. Fitness is the name of the game, coupled with self-discipline and eating the right food.

No More Mr Nice Guy

'Challenge the judo black belt from the self-defence exhibition!'
Ringside Punter

At the end of the Second World War I was drafted into the RAF. I chose this branch of the services because I had been a member of the Air Cadets from 1940 and it was during this time I learnt to box. It was a sport that I thoroughly enjoyed and did not mind taking a punch or two. As a matter of fact I thought I was pretty handy with my fists and fancied myself as a future middleweight champion. That was until my commanding officer invited the British champion, Paddy Ryan, to give an exhibition of boxing and training techniques. The CO invited volunteers to step into the ring for two minutes with Paddy. Needless to say, no one did, except me, foolishly fancying my chances. Although Paddy was wearing 10 oz training gloves, designed not to hurt, I received the biggest pasting of my life and endured the longest two minutes, but it taught me the vast difference between amateurs and professionals.

My interest then turned to the martial arts, judo, karate and aikido and I was then posted to Gütersloh in Germany, and then seconded to the army barracks at Paderborn as an instructor.

One evening, after taking a self-defence class, I was rolling up the mat when I was approached by a couple of German ex-prisoners of war who still worked at the camp. They asked me if I would leave the mat down as they were representing their town in an amateur wrestling competition and needed to practise some holds. I agreed, on the condition that I might stay and watch, but eventually joined them on the mat and continued to do so for many months. I realised that judo and wrestling were a good combination of skills since many of the throws and holds could be adapted to work together very successfully.

Upon demob in 1948, I returned to Stockport. I was then married to Betty and we settled down in a little cottage in Marple. I'd known her since 1944 when I'd met her at the engineering factory I worked in, setting the lathes up for making inoculation syringes. I was called up to the RAF shortly after. We remained married for forty years, with our daughter Leslie arriving in 1943. Money was short and jobs were scarce. I worked during the day, but for three evenings a week I taught martial arts at a club I had opened in Marple.

I set the club up at premises a few doors away from where I lived. Lilly Low was a lady that ran a shop with a tearoom on the corner but she closed it down – it was no more than a big shed and it had stood empty for a while. I asked her if I could rent the hut off her and she agreed. I bought several ex-forces mattresses from the Army and Navy store and I put them down on the hut floor and then advertised. I soon had about thirty or forty pupils attending. Lilly got fed up with the noise so I had to find a new venue to teach at.

The British Legion in Marple had a big room that was never used. I bought more mattresses for the extra space so that they covered the entire floor area. I got a cover put over and tightened it every night – it was a cracking mat. I began teaching the police at Warren Street and when they closed that down, the police came to my club and began teaching themselves the art of self-defence. We charged peanuts and it barely covered the expenses of the club, but, of course, money was never the driving force.

One Sunday afternoon I was invited to a demonstration of judo and aikido in Chester. Kenshiro Abbe, an Eighth Dan Japanese Samurai, was touring England teaching and grading. I invited him to my club and to my delight he accepted. He was very impressed with the facilities of the club and the enthusiasm of the members, who were a mixed group of males and females; their ages ranged from teenager to pensioners. In exchange for use of the club he offered to teach me his personal techniques or at least some of them. During his visit he stayed with us at our cottage and I would watch in amazement at this gentle, paper-folding judo master who could kill a man with one hand, as he sat with my two-year-old daughter, Lesley, on the carpet crooning to her in Japanese.

One night, he was demonstrating self-defence using karate and Aikido when he asked me to go and find him a piece of wood. In the spare room, I found a billiard table leg. It was about three inches thick and carved from solid mahogany. Believing it would be impossible for anyone to break it, even with a sledgehammer, I handed it over for a joke.

Without batting an eyelid, he placed it across two chairs and, with the edge of his hand, he broke it clean in half. Quite incredible.

Kenshiro was a gentleman, but he was also one of the highest-graded men in Japan. He was the chief instructor for the Tokyo police and also the chief instructor in the Japanese Army. I recall taking him to the pictures one night and I was keen to avoid watching a war movie, for obvious reasons. We all settled down to watch this film and the very first scene showed a woman and a girl running towards a hut. The next thing, these Japanese soldiers appeared and shot them down – I nearly died of embarrassment, but Kenshiro never twitched a muscle.

To look at him, you would never have guessed he was a master of martial arts. He was completely bald and looked a little podgy – if he was sat in a pub and somebody fancied a bit of trouble, he'd be the one they picked on because he looked so benevolent. But when he stripped, what a physique! If someone had picked on him, they'd have been thrown straight through the window – he was unbelievable and could kill a man in seconds with one fairly simple move.

Before he left to return home he named my club The Shin-Bu-Kan which, in Japanese, translates as 'True Fighting House'. Unfortunately we never met again and I was sad to hear that he had died suddenly at the age of fifty-two years. However, his teaching had opened up my expertise considerably and in October 1960, I gained my black belt First Dan. I learned discipline from him and his influence stayed with me throughout my career.

Shortly after this, the Stockport Education Authority approached me with an offer to become their chief instructor. This involved providing instructors for youth clubs and evening institutes in the area. The demand was quite heavy, judo being a very popular sport at the time.

Periodically I would grade the students, usually at schools or youth clubs. This would include youngsters taking judo as part of their Duke of Edinburgh Award Scheme. It was a thoroughly rewarding and enjoyable experience to witness their wholehearted dedication.

Judo was known as the gentle art, but some of the young students were far from gentle. I was grading a group of youngsters one evening at a school in Stockport. The mat was exceptionally small and had been placed about 4 ft from the stage in the assembly hall. One of the lads threw his opponent with a well-executed drawing ankle technique and a good deal of brute strength. He shot across the mat and went skidding along the polished floor, crashing into the base of the stage. A little while later, one of the pupils pointed out to me that water was seeping from behind the panelling. Sliding it back, I discovered two large tropical fish tanks. One held fairly large fish and the other tiny ones, and it was these that were threshing about, gasping for air as the broken tank emptied on to the floor.

Without more ado everyone started to scoop them up and drop them into the other tank but to our horror, in a feeding frenzy, the bigger fish swooped on the little ones gobbling them up.

I had some explaining to do the next morning to the headmaster. He was not very pleased and I was never invited back.

A father of one of my pupils owned a nightclub in Stockport and he asked me if I would put on an exhibition of self-defence during the interval of the following Wednesday night professional wrestling bill. This proved to be very popular and another club owner, ex-professional Bill (Man Mountain) Benny, approached me to give the same exhibition at his nightclub in Levenshulme, Manchester. I brought along four members of my Shin-Bu-Kan club and once again the evening was a runaway success.

The final wrestling bout of the evening was between a local lad named Tommy Jacks and a Dutchman named Peto Van Scott. Scott was the heavier and appeared huge in comparison. In spite of liberal use of his fist, he did not have his own way thanks to the deceptive speed and strength of his lighter opponent. Jacks bounced him around the ring to the cheers of the crowd.

This infuriated Scott. He claimed Jacks and slammed his head into the corner post, back-elbowing the referee when he had attempted to restrain him. Scott was immediately disqualified and the crowd were incensed. One man leapt to his feet shouting insults at Scott and then daring him to challenge the judo black belt from the self-defence exhibition. Scott screamed back at him that he could take me any time and I would not last five minutes against him.

Bill Benny, quick to size up the situation, realised that he could pack the club the following week if I would agree to accept the challenge. He offered me double the fee he had paid me for the exhibition so I snatched his hand off. I thought that brains would overcome brawn, but it was not that easy.

True to Benny's prediction I arrived to a packed club feeling more than a little nervous but quietly confident. I knew that the ring floors were very hard in contrast to the judo mats, but I had had a lot of experience over the years of breaking a fall. What I had not experienced were the body slams and suplexes, which are far different from the judo throwing techniques. In a body slam your opponent slides an arm around your shoulder and another arm between your legs. He then lifts you above his head and slams you as hard as he can on to the hard ring floor. With a suplex your head is grabbed by both hands and pulled down to tuck under the armpit – not a pleasant experience. Your opponent will then drop on his back bringing you over like a whiplash and if you don't know how to fall properly it will drive every ounce of breath out of your body.

That evening in my dressing room, I changed into my judogi and then sat wondering what the hell I had let myself in for; but I still remained confident. As expected the hall was a complete sell-out. As I approached the ring the crowd were roaring at me to screw his head off, break both his legs and then his arms.

To say that I was overwhelmed would be an understatement. Never before had I experienced such hostility, not to myself but to my opponent who, ignoring the abuse thrown at him, climbed into the ring. As the bell rang for the first round, I approached the centre of the ring and according to the etiquette of judo and, as a gesture of honour, I naively bowed to him, whereupon he promptly grabbed me by the hair and threw me across the ring, then hauled me to my feet and body slammed me.

Unprepared for such an onslaught, I climbed to my feet. I was suplexed, pulled up again and unceremoniously thrown over the ropes, out of the ring within the first two minutes. Although the crowd booed him and cheered me, I felt that they expected that he would make mincemeat of me. I climbed back on to the ring apron thinking, I've had enough this. If this is how he wants to play it, so be it. He reached over the ropes to grab my hair again, but instead I claimed his hand and using an aikido technique I threw him halfway across the ring. Sensing that something was brewing the crowd began to urge me on. Remembering the moves that I had practised with the German lads, and drawing on good knowledge of ju jitsu, I bounced him around the ring until the bell rang for the end of the first round.

I returned to my corner thinking 'No more Mr Nice Guy'. When the bell rang for the second round I was ready for him. It was three rounds of avoiding, if I could, his head and knees. I suffered a few bruises and although he twisted my left arm and attempted to kick me in the stomach, I finally caught his leg, kicked his other from under him and, applying a painful lock on his knee, gained the one submission needed to win the match. It was a hard, bruising, but exhilarating experience. The crowd loved it and so did Bill Benny, but more importantly it led to many more bouts up and down the country, and set me on course for the next twenty or so years.

The Sad Demise of the Great Mitsi Moto

'The Great Mitsi Moto is as English as roast beef!'
Newspaper headline

Choosing a name for myself was a problem. For a while I used my own name, Alf Margetts, but some promoters didn't seem to get the hang of it and I would find myself billed as Alf Margate, Margott, all sorts of interpretations. So I decided that since I wrestled as a judoka, I would call myself the Great Mitsi Moto; and to create further intrigue I would refrain from speaking. If fans asked me for my autograph I just signed but never spoke.

This harmonised very well, because at the time a programme on television was about a Tibetan monk (played by David Carradine) who left his monastery and each week would come to the aid of some poor unfortunate. His martial arts skills saved the day for the victim, and as the show ended he would pick up his pack and wander off into the distance (until next week).

This worked very well for me and I began to build a reputation for myself. One evening I was invited to wrestle on a bill in Manchester, with all the proceeds going to charity. It was a very successful night and the local press were there to interview the wrestlers and two stars from *Coronation Street* – namely Peter Adamson and Jack Howarth, who had come to raffle footballs and cricket bats donated by the Manchester clubs.

Everyone on the bill was interviewed except me, since I spoke no English. So after I had showered, I jumped into my car and drove home. However, one reporter followed me. The following issue of the paper gave an account of the evening, the amount raised and the interviews. Then in bold type she had written: **'The Great Mitsi Moto is as English as roast beef!'** She had put all my details in the paper; my real name and address and even the area. So that was the end of Mitsi Moto.

I changed into white judo gear, and when I signed with Joint Promotions, again another promoter got my name wrong and billed me as Al Marquette. That seemed to stick in their minds, so for the rest of my career that was my name.

After my first appearance on television that same woman reporter had the brass neck to knock on my door at home and ask for an interview. It gave me great pleasure to say, 'Sorry my dear,' or words to that effect.

On a warm summer's evening in 1968, at an open-air wrestling promotion in St Helens, Lancashire, I was matched against Pete Linberg; one of this country's strongest men but I managed to gain two submissions to win the match. This occasion is etched on my memory for two reasons. The first is being caught on the ear by a forearm smash from Pete resulting in a cauliflower ear which I have to this day; second, and more importantly, upon my returning to the marquee, which served as a dressing room, sitting on a table waiting for me was a man I had seen around before. He introduced himself as Billy Hargreaves, an ex-wrestler and a partner of Jack Atherton; another ex-wrestler from the 'Blood Tub' days and one of the North's top wrestling promoters. Apparently Jack had seen me before my professional wrestling debut demonstrating self-defence techniques, and suggested that Billy came to St Helens to watch the bout.

'Would you be interested in signing a contract with Joint Promotions, lad?' he asked. 'It will mean the big halls and TV appearances.'

A meeting was arranged for the following week at a gym in Leeds. Jack Atherton and several more of the top promoters were also present. Also in the gym at the same time, training with Shozo Kobayashi, a huge Japanese heavyweight, was Jimmy Saville. He was doing press ups with his customary cigar clenched between his teeth. Jimmy loved the game and had had a few bouts as a middleweight, the most notable against the ex-world champion, Gentleman Jim Lewis. He took a lot of punishment and he displayed a lot of guts, and he was lucky not to leave them all over the ring floor.

After being introduced to Alan Dennison, a top TV wrestler, we went into the ring for a five-minute pull. They must have liked what they saw because the terms of the contract were agreed, and I was signed up immediately.

Within two weeks I was given my first television appearance against Alan Colbeck at the Civic Hall, Sheffield. When I arrived, the hall was a hive of activity with electricians, camera crew, television executives and lighting engineers buzzing around setting up their equipment. All week my stomach had been churning at the prospect of being seen on television by millions of people but, paradoxically, when I observed all the frenetic energy going on I found to my amazement that I felt calm and in control.

Sharing the bill that evening were Thunder Sugiyama versus Henri Pierlot and Pancho Zapata versus Jeff Kaye.

Kent Walton came to my dressing room for some information regarding my family, how had I been approached by Joint Promotions, and anything that would be of interest to the viewing public. He explained what I could expect from my first televised appearance and how the lights, because they generated so much heat, could affect your stamina. Also not to allow the cameras to distract me thus, losing concentration; all excellent advice and very much appreciated. Kent was very friendly and easy to talk to, but he always held back, never becoming 'one of the boys' – always remaining impartial.

Although I was nervous on that first occasion, I did have a very good bout against the European welterweight kingpin, Alan Colbeck. He was a rough handful, resorting to tactics falling short of the rules at times, also a few kidney punches delivered on the blind side of the referee. In true judoka style, I wrestled in my bare feet, over the years hardening them by soaking them in baths of brine along with my hands, so when he tried to hurt me by stamping on them as hard as he could, he was wasting his time. In the fourth round his frustration got the better of him and he was disqualified for refusing to break an illegal hold.

Later, watching the bout on television, I was pleased with Kent's commentary. He was very complimentary about me and continued to be so with all my bouts on television. He considered that tag matches were not for me and advised me to stick to single bouts, which were more suited to my style.

My bare feet came in for a lot of stick during the bouts and that was all right by me. I considered it to be part and parcel of the game. But when a member of the public tries it on, that is a different ball game.

I was wrestling at a charity match at Manchester University and the ring was placed about six feet away from the stage and some of the students were seated near the front edge. I had my feet stamped on several times by my opponent, which I took in my stride. As I left the ring, one of the students, obviously showing off in front of his girlfriend, leapt off the stage landing with both feet on my foot.

Grinning at the girls, he said to me sarcastically, 'I'm very sorry. I haven't hurt your foot, have I?'

'No,' I replied, 'and I'll tell you why you haven't hurt my foot, because if you had, you'd be flat on your back by now.'

Sheepishly, he climbed back onto the stage, not knowing how close he'd come to having that smirk wiped off his face.

I had been wrestling for about six months for Joint Promotions when I first met Steve Logan. The dressing rooms at the King's Hall, Belle Vue, were just small cubicles without doors and I was sitting in my judo gear waiting to enter the ring when Steve Logan and Mick McManus, who were topping the bill as a tag team, walked down the corridor and Logan remarked in his Cockney accent, 'Hey Mick, there's a bloke here in his pyjamas!'

I ignored him and a couple of minutes later he returned and, standing in front of me, said, 'Is your name Marquette?'

I nodded yes.

'Do you know you're at the Royal Albert Hall next week?'

Again I nodded yes.

He went on, 'Do you know who you're wrestling?'

I shook my head to indicate that I did not.

'Well, you're wrestling me and if I were you, I wouldn't buy any long playing records.'

This really put my teeth on edge, but I ignored him again and he walked away.

The following Wednesday I arrived at Stockport Station to catch the midday train to London. The platform was packed with commuters and I realised that it was going to be a long and uncomfortable journey, as indeed it was. At least I managed to find a seat; but I had to keep my bag on my knees as there was no room for it on the overhead rack.

Leaving Euston Station I headed for the nearest taxi rank; but again, there was a queue, and by the time I had reached my turn, my mood had plummeted. However, the taxi driver was in a cheerful mood. 'Where to, Guv?' he asked.

'The Royal Albert Hall,' I answered him, sinking gratefully into the seat.

'That's a Northern accent isn't it? Is this your first visit to London?'

I told him that I had been once before in 1945, at the end of the war. I was on a twenty-four-hour pass from the RAF base at Greenham Common Newbury, where I had been stationed. He then proceeded to point out some well known buildings and landmarks, I began to relax and appreciate his Cockney good humour. He added that it was his good fortune that I was going to the Royal Albert Hall, because I was his last passenger and then he was off to the wrestling there.

He went on to say, 'If that's where you are going, I hope you have got a ticket, because it's a complete sell-out, and the touts are commanding all sorts of silly prices.'

'I don't need a ticket,' I replied. 'I'm on the bill.'

Our eyes met in the rear-view mirror, and he stared at me in disbelief.

'Why! Who the bleeding hell are you?'

'Al Marquette.'

'Al Marquette,' he repeated, 'you're on with Logan, and he's twice your size – he'll bleeding well kill you.'

Again our eyes met in the mirror, I raised my eyebrows with a 'we'll see' gesture.

'I'll tell you what, Guv, if you're still in one piece after the bout, come up to the bar during the interval. All the lads will be there, and we'll buy you a drink.'

Grinning all over his face he concluded, 'You'll need it.'

I raised my hand as he sped away, and turning, I looked up at the wonderful building in front of me, perfectly rotund and with its beautiful domed roof, I thought of the other people who have performed there, and how they must have felt when they too, possibly standing in the very same spot as me, looked at that magnificent building.

My attention was then taken by the billboard advertising the evening's bouts. It was headed:

The 1969 Wrestling Spectacular
Return Contest
Between Mick McManus and Les Kellet
Jackie Pallo v George Kidd
– Lightweight Champion of the World

The Battle of the Giants
– Jean Ferre v Big Bruno Elrington
Wild Ian Campbell v Mike Marino
The Iron Man Steve Logan v Al Marquette
Lee Thomas v Ivan Penzecoff

Tag Match
The Silent Ones: Mike Eagen and Harry Kendall
v
The Untouchables: Leon Arras and Lee Sharron.

What a bill – small wonder that is was a sell-out. Hundreds of people were milling about outside the hall, trying to buy tickets from the touts at hugely inflated prices.

I felt the first flicker of apprehension, not because of who I was wrestling, but because it was the first time I had appeared there and knowing that the fans were knowledgeable, and only appreciated the best. They were used to the big names from all over the world and did not suffer mediocre wrestling gladly.

As I entered the hall the spectacular lighting illuminated the domed ceiling. The tiered seating graduated down to the ringside. Red carpets led from the dressing rooms down to the ring. There was the loud hum of voices from the 6,000 spectators eagerly awaiting the first bout to begin; and finally, the sudden hush as the hall lights dimmed and the powerful ring lights lit up the roped square, all adding to my unease.

The hall was heaving and I could feel the excitement and anticipation of the huge crowd. Billy Dale, the Managing Director of Dale-Martin Promotions, advised me to stand at the back of the hall for a little while to get used to the atmosphere.

I shared a dressing room with George Kidd and Mike Marino and they put me at my ease by chatting until I was due in the ring. As I stepped out of the dressing room, barefoot in my white judogi and coveted black belt the carpeted aisle seemed to stretch for miles. A thick pall of cigar and cigarette smoke hung under the glaring ring lights and, as I climbed the steps to the ring apron, polite applause greeted me. As I ducked through the ropes, I could feel the eyes of thousands of fans upon me. Although a familiar figure in the rings of my native North, I was here an unknown quantity to most of the southern fans.

The fanfare rang out; a spotlight focused on the dressing room door and my famous opponent emerged. The Iron Man, Steve Logan, black hair hanging over his scowling face, a towel draped over his bare shoulders, strode menacingly down to the ring. 'The Entry of the Gladiators' was blaring out over the loudspeakers merging with the hissing and booing of the spectators – the man they loved to hate.

The bell sounded for the first round and Logan ran across the ring in his usual aggressive style to deliver his famous forearm smash. The polite applause changed to wholehearted cheering that nearly took the roof off when I dropped him on the seat of his black trunks – three times in the first thirty seconds.

The response was unbelievable. My ears were popping with the roar from the crowd. Billy Dale told me later that he came rushing from the dressing room thinking that some sort of a calamity had occurred.

Logan's aggressive style suited me down to the ground, and time and time again I used it to throw him all over the ring. The crowd were on the edge of their seats urging me to finish him off. Oh, that it was that easy. I was giving away between 2 and 3 st. in weight, plus there was his huge strength and I knew I would have to move fast and use all my skills to keep out of trouble. He caught my left hand in a powerful knuckle grip but as he leaned forward to force me down to the canvas I hit him with a right-hand chop that lifted him clean off his feet in a forward somersault and he landed flat on his back.

I thought he'd never get up from that, but he did. He was looking very groggy so I moved in to claim him and he hit me with a forearm smash that nearly took my head off. As I climbed back to my feet he body slammed me, pulled me back to my feet by my hair and then hurled me into a corner post. He then rushed across the ring to deliver a forearm smash but I ducked away, caught hold of his wrists and pulled his hands and elbows into a Japanese arm lock. It is a move that I was taught many years ago. With hindsight I should have kicked his legs from under him and pinned him for a fall but instead I released him from the lock.

As the bell sounded for the fourth round I turned from my corner and Logan had run across the ring to claim me I ducked under his arm, tripped him and he shot through the ropes into the front seats. The ringsiders laid into him with fists and feet so to help him back into the ring quickly, I lifted the middle rope, but Logan, being Logan, took advantage of this.

He spun me round to the blind side of the referee and punched me in the kidneys with his fist. As I fell back he pinned me for the only fall needed to win the bout – a very controversial decision. The crowd were incensed and as Logan left the ring he was attacked by some very irate ringsiders. In the melee that ensued he knocked one man unconscious.

Back in the dressing room I could hear the commotion going on in Logan's. He was ranting and raving about the referee, the fans who attacked him, and particularly about me for using unorthodox techniques. Although we did not meet again that night, I wrestled him a few times over the years and he never changed, always a very aggressive and hard man.

However, for me, that night was a triumphant London debut and led to many more appearances at the Royal Albert Hall. Incidentally, I did have that drink with my taxi friend and his mates and later he drove me back to Euston Station, free of charge.

The platform was crowded with people waiting for trains and

I guessed they were the fans from the Royal Albert Hall. To my amazement I found myself surrounded by people congratulating me, slapping me on the back and asking me to sign their autograph books and programmes.

I was overwhelmed by the unexpected response and I realised that I had reached the first pinnacle of my wrestling career. I was also overwhelmed by an article written in the monthly magazine *The Wrestler* by reporter Russell Plummer. I quote.

> The dust having finally settled from the Royal Albert Hall end of season spectacular a month ago, the lasting memory of the fans will not be of established stars such as Mick McManus, Les Kellet or Jackie Pallo but the slender white jacketed figure of wrestler Al Marquette.
>
> Virtually unknown outside his native north, quiet unassuming Al stepped into the limelight before six thousand of the country's discerning fans and left to the sort of ovation usually reserved for visiting international stars and then only those of the highest merit.
>
> Few men have so quickly won their way into the hearts of the crowd and although beaten on a very dubious decision by the considerably heavier Steve Logan for Marquette, long an unsung star of the independent halls, this was indeed a triumphant London debut.

All in the Family

'Is that you, Marquette? Bloody hell, I thought you would be dead by now!'
Brian Glover

Most of the wrestlers developed their skills in the gyms and competing in amateur bouts up and down the country. However, a few had the added advantage of being the sons of famous fathers.

Charlie and Brian Glover

A very popular wrestler whom I had watched many times at the Blood Tub and Belle Vue was the masked Red Devil, a bluff Yorkshireman of thickset build He was not averse to bending the rules and could incite the crowd almost to a frenzy as he fouled his opponents on many occasions, especially if they attempted to unmask him. As the rule book lays down, any masked man who had been beaten was expected to reveal his identity. Charlie Glover, for that was his name, had never been beaten but was so familiar that, as he climbed into the ring in his red gear and mask, people would call out, 'Hiya Charlie'. A tribute to his wrestling prowess was that in all the years in the ring, not one of his opponents had managed to unmask him.

Charlie's son was Brian Glover, a heavyweight who fought under the name of Leon Arras. Brian was a full-time school teacher who wrestled in his spare time. Like father, like son, he was a mixture of villain and hero. On the few occasions that I fought him, the bouts were fast and furious and if the referee ever called one of his moves into question, Brian would shout, 'I know the rules!' to which the crowd would echo with a roar, 'He knows the rules ref.' This became his slogan and he would repeat it at every bout.

His entry into films and television work came about when a film crew came to the school where he taught to shoot a scene for the classic film, *Kes*. As he watched the actors auditioning for the role of a sports master trying to control a team of unruly boys, Brian remarked to the director, 'It's no use treating 'em with kid gloves, you've got to show 'em who's boss,' or words to that effect. He was then challenged to demonstrate how he would control them and apparently was so good, the part was offered to him. He never looked back. Television work followed and he was to be seen in productions such as *Porridge* where he played a braindead prisoner alongside Ronnie Barker and Richard Beckinsale. He also played a tough guy in many films and also toured with the Royal Shakespeare Company. But I think it was his voice that most people will remember, particularly the television advert for Tetley tea bags.

I had not seen Brian since I retired from wrestling in 1977. One morning I was reading my paper at home when the telephone rang and an unmistakable voice said, 'Is that you Marquette?'

I said it was and the voice continued, 'Bloody hell, I thought you would be dead by now!' – typical Brian.

Apparently he was recording an interview for breakfast television at the Manchester studios and went on to recall the time he was writing a play about wrestling. One of the characters was a judo expert and Brian had wanted some advice on the Japanese names of judo throws. I wrote out the Nage-No-Kata, which are the fifteen formal throwing techniques, and gave them to him. A fortnight later we met again in the dressing room at one of the venues.

'I'm sorry, Al,' he said, 'but in the script I took the mickey a bit. The judo lad was showing off with his fancy Japanese names, so the lads throw him through the window!'

'That's OK, Brian,' I replied. 'I knew full well you would take liberties along those lines, so that's why I gave you all the wrong names!'

The air was blue for the next few minutes since he had already sent the play to be published. I let him seethe for a while before admitting that I, too, had been taking the mickey and the names were genuine. We agreed that the next time he was in Manchester we would meet for a meal to recall old times. However, this was not to be, for sadly Brian died suddenly, a few months later. I couldn't believe it – he was a real talent.

Jack Pye and Dominic

Jack Pye was, without doubt, the most diabolical ring villain of his day. Over 6 ft in height and dressed in a black vest and tights he strutted around the ring holding the top rope, and hurling abuse in response to the spectators' catcalls. They hated him, and yet he packed the halls wherever he appeared. Chin on his chest, he glared at them, daring anyone stupid enough to chance their arm.

Some of the bouts he had with his contemporaries, Francis Gregory and Bert Assirati, had to be seen to be believed. They were so contentious it was a miracle that any one of them left the ring without serious injury.

His son, Dominic, was exactly like his father. His weight and build were the same, he wore the same black vest and tights, and his aggression was the same. He too, would prowl the ring, verbally abusing the fans and taking liberties with the referee. However, unlike his father, whose face over the years had taken some stick, and whose looks were battered to say the least, Dominic seemed to manage to maintain his; he was a very handsome and imposing man.

He was also a successful businessman in his own right as well as co-sharing a night club with Jack in Blackpool. It was at this club that a man, having parked his sports car outside the main door, and after refusing repeated requests to move it, brought the wrath of Dominic down upon his head. Taking hold of the car, Dominic completely tipped it, unaided, on to its side, demonstrating his enormous strength and convincing the chap that he perhaps should heed such advice in future.

I never had the pleasure of wrestling him (thankfully) but I remember judging a beauty contest with him in the sixties. It must have been nerve-racking enough for the young ladies, but to be confronted with two bruisers like us must have scared the living daylights out of them. Apart from being a big man, he had a big voice as well, and as the questions boomed out, their replies came back as strangled little squeaks. Kneecaps knocking, lips quivering as they tried to fix a smile, the girls lined up before us. I do not enjoy judging beauty contests simply because I think they all deserve to win, and I confess to chickening out and voting with the majority.

Another contest I judged along with Pye was the Miss Cheshire Rose in 1964. Fortunately we had the previous year's winner with us and we were able to bow to her superior knowledge.

I liked Dominic. We got on, as they say, and I was very sorry to learn, not long after, that he had been killed in a shooting accident with a faulty shotgun.

Vic Hesselle and sons Bert and Vic

Vic Hesselle, real name Vic Faulkner, was one of my heroes from the Blood Tub era. He was born in Bolton, Lancashire in 1914 and became interested in wrestling at a very early age. In 1935 he won the Lancashire amateur championships at both Middle and Light Heavyweight limits.

He joined the army in 1940 and quickly became sergeant PT instructor in the 6th Airborne Paratroop Regiment. On demob in 1946 he joined the ranks of professional wrestlers and immediately became a firm favourite with the Belle Vue fans. He had one of the finest physiques in the game and it was inevitable that his two sons, Bert and Vic, would follow in his footsteps, becoming the famous Royal Brothers tag team. They were both members of the Bolton Harriers gym and became proficient amateur wrestlers.

At the time, Bert was training, would you believe, in ladies' hairdressing – colouring and styling – and he has his Guild Certificate from the Hairdressing Registration Council. Fortunately for his thousands of fans, wrestling won the day. Vic senior continued Bert's training on the back lawn of their home until he was ready to turn professional at the age of eighteen.

He decided to wrestle under the name of Bert Royal in 1953 because it was the year of the Queen's Coronation. He gained valuable experience wrestling in France and Belgium, beating the cream of Europe's middleweights, and on returning to England he became the British and European middleweight champion. Along with Vic senior he helped young Vic to reach professional standard and Vic's rise to fame was phenomenal. His spectacular techniques and agility assured him top billing at the major venues across Britain. They formed the Fabulous Royal Brothers tag team and became firm favourites with the television viewers.

After thirty years in the ring they have both hung up their boots and became area sales managers in the wines and spirits trade. Vic is still working but Bert retired in 2002. I would not be surprised to hear he is interested in politics again. He was elected to the council in his own borough in 1967 as a Liberal candidate.

Bert and I meet up every few weeks for a pint and a chat about the old days.

Francis St Clair Gregory, Roy and Tony St Clair

Francis St Clair Gregory was the famous father of the equally famous Roy and Tony St Clair. He began his wrestling career in Cornwall, winning six Cornish-style championships at different weights. During the late thirties he turned professional and moved to Manchester, training at Ernie Riley's gym in Wigan. He retired in the late fifties and became the landlord of a hotel near Manchester. Incidentally, Francis appeared as top of the bill against Mike Marino on the very first show to be televised, in November 1955.

He coached his two sons as amateurs and when they both turned professional, they continued their training at the Wryton Stadium in Bolton. They reached their star billing both as individuals and as the Saints tag team.

Tony is still wrestling in Germany and also runs a school for amateurs who hope to turn professional. Roy has followed in his father's footsteps into the licensed trade.

Alf Robinson, son Jackie Robinson and nephew Billy

Boxing in the early 1930s was a sport that attracted only the hardest and the fittest – Nel Tarleton, Freddie Mills, Len Harvey, Jack McAvoy, Jackie Brown, Paddy Ryan and one of the hardest and fittest, Alf Robinson. Some of the so-called champions of today would not have lasted one round against these dedicated fighters.

Alf fought and beat all comers on his way to the top, winning the British Belle Vue Heavyweight Belt in 1934 and then going on to beat Norman Baines to win the Lonsdale Trophy at the Wembley Arena in 1937. A very prestigious award.

After being demobbed from the army in 1945 he turned to his other favourite sport – wrestling – topping the bill at the Ardwick Stadium, Belle Vue and other great venues throughout Europe. He very soon built up the same reputation he had forged as a boxer, beating most of the top heavyweights including such names as Jack and Dominic Pye, Jack Atherton and the Farmer's Boy.

Billy

Inspired by his uncle, Robinson trained as a wrestler at the Failsworth Sports Club, winning many trophies. After turning professional in the 1960s, he became one of the greatest heavyweights this country has ever produced, winning the British Heavyweight Championship.

He was powerfully built and about 6 ft in height with dark curly hair. One of his favourite moves was his own execution of a step-over leg lock, a devastating move guaranteed to bring a submission or a broken leg.

Following a successful tour to Japan in the 1970s where he beat the cream of the top Japanese wrestlers, he took America by storm claiming the World Championship by beating Dory Funk. So successful was he in the States that he did not return to England, making his home there teaching youngsters the art of wrestling on his own weekly show on television.

Jackie

Keeping up the family tradition, Jackie Robinson followed his father and cousin into the wrestling ring. Training at the same Failsworth Club as his cousin, he made a name for himself in the amateur ranks before turning professional in 1968.

With his family background he could hardly fail to become the best lightweight in the country, winning the European Championship in the late 1960s. Although smaller and lighter in build than his father and cousin, he was nonetheless extremely fast and agile beating many of the top European light and middleweight champions. His skills were appreciated by his many fans.

I wrestled Jackie several times over the years, including a television bout, and in fact my last appearance as a professional wrestler was against him at the Stockport Town Hall in 1977. Although he is no longer involved with the sport, he is managing director of his own company, a miniature theme park on the promenade at Morecombe, Lancashire, comprising go carts, swings, helter-skelters and enough entertainment to keep the kids happy all day long.

Stan Rylands and Bobby Ryan

The name of Stan Rylands was perhaps better know as a referee – he had wrestled as a professional – but I knew him more as an official in the ring rather than an opponent. He was the main referee at Victoria Hall at Hanley, Stoke-on-Trent and, believe me, you had to be good to survive there.

It wasn't only the wrestlers he had to keep his eye on but the ladies sitting at the ringside – upset them and they could be more dangerous that the men in the ring! A good ref should keep control of a bout and Stan was one of the best.

His son, Bobby, was keen on becoming a speedway star rather than following in his father's footsteps and was backed up by his uncle, who owned a number of bikes. He also had a farm that included a track, so Bobby's mind was set.

While at the gyms, he met many of the North's biggest names in wrestling: there was Bert Royal, Vic Faulkner, Johnny Saint, Marty Jones and one of his great heroes, Bobo Matu.

To his surprise, he did like the sport and within a year was ready to turn professional, wrestling under the name of Bobby Ryan. One of the North's more colourful promoters, Jack Atherton, put him on the bill at Warden in Worcestershire, pitting against Cyanide Sid Cooper.

Atherton said to the youngster, 'Now, lad, dun't tha be lettin' me darn, else I'll see thee does'na enter the ring again.'

Bobby lost!

Two falls to nil in a three-round contest – he was just too nervous. Somehow, though, Jack must have liked what he saw because Bobby's career went from strength to strength, winning both the European and British championships. His passion for speedway never diminished, however, and whenever he wrestled at Belle Vue, he nipped over to the track and chatted with the Aces.

He recalled one evening, telling the promoter he was just 'nipping over' to the speedway for half an hour. Fifteen minutes later, it was announced over the PA system, 'Bobby Ryan, get your ass over to King's Hall, you're in the ring in fifteen minutes.' It turned out one of the wrestlers had been delayed and his bout had been brought forward.

After many successful years, Max Crabtree, the promoter brother of Big Daddy, rang him inviting Bobby to partner the big man in the ring. This was too big an opportunity to miss since it meant big venues, plenty of television coverage and more money.

The downside, however, was that all his opponents were huge men – Judd Harris, Mel Kirk and Pat Roach were prime examples, with Harris and Kirk weighing in at 22 st. each.

Bobby was unable to do much apart from butting them with his belly and the body slams and beatings soon took their toll. Finally, after being hospitalised with a throat injury, he realised he was taking all the bumps and Big Daddy all the applause. Indeed, his father's wise words: 'The wasp makes the sting, the bee makes the honey; the Lightweights do the work and the Heavies make the money' had helped him decide this latest injury would be his last as a tag partner for Big Daddy, or anyone else for that matter.

October 16 1982 was the day that changed Bobby's life for ever. He was scheduled to fight at the Victoria Hall, but his father died that same day. He was devastated – his father had been his main supporter and severest critic. So, ringing the promoter, he pulled out, put away his boots and never wrestled again.

Now a devoted family man, he is totally involved in managing his own soft-drinks company.

Grand Halls, Bear Pits and Loaded Handbags

Different halls and venues held different memories for all of us and one of my favourite halls was the King's Hall, Belle Vue, Manchester. It was fairly close to my home and as a boy I would see the posters displayed on the advertising hoardings for the following Saturday night wrestling bill: St Clair Gregory, Tommy the Demon, Les Kellet, the Angel, Joe Critchley, Jack and Dominic Pye and all the other big names of the day.

The posters would conjure up a vivid picture of the glamour and excitement of the wrestlers striding down from the dressing rooms to the ring. Some would be flamboyantly dressed – elaborate dressing gowns, colourful trunks and boots, Billy Two Rivers with his fantastic feathered headdress and moccasin boots and Joe Critchley with his tray of roses for the ladies. In contrast were the villainous Jack and Dominic Pye wearing all black: tights, trunks and vests.

I remember also the powerful ring lights, highlighting the white canvas floor and the red and blue corner posts with the wrestlers standing in their corners waiting for the first bell and hoping they would leave without injury.

I remember the tremendous thrill I felt the first time I saw my name on a Belle Vue poster, and the encouragement I received from the Belle Vue audience. Absolute magic. It was also the home of speedway racing, which had a huge following of fans. One thing you had to remember though was never to stand near the bends, simply because as the riders' machines slid into the curves, a spray of choking dust and cinders rained down on the unsuspecting; usually newcomers to the sport.

Before television, Continental holidays, theme parks and all the rest of modern-time attractions, Belle Vue was a Mecca for the family as well as the younger generations. As a matter of fact, just after the Second World War, couples actually went to Belle Vue to spend their honeymoon – married in the morning and spending the rest of the day at the fairground or playing at the many side stalls and attractions. There was something for everyone, from the swings and merry-go-rounds for the very young, to the stomach-churning rides on the 'bobs' for the more adventurous. You could hear the girls' screams all over the park as the carriages clanked up the very steep inclines to the top, only to plunge headlong down the almost vertical rails.

There were plenty of shooting galleries and coconut shies, and one sideshow that always drew a lot of attention from the lads, was a scantily dressed young lady sitting on a seat suspended above a large tub of water with a target above her head. If you struck bullseye, she was plunged into the water and a prize was won. Fortunately she was protected from the 'no balls' by a net. There were also other great rides such as the big dipper, the ferris wheel, the caterpillar – this one always invited a large group of male bystanders since a wind machine blew up the girls' skirts and, as they struggled to keep their modesty, a hood descended over them, and all attention was withdrawn until the hood drew back again, and a final blast rekindled interest.

There was so much to do, but if you wanted a more sedate attraction a ride around the park on an elephant or a camel was yours for the asking. Only the unsuspecting and very young sat behind the elephant; the less gullible sat out of range because the chances were that the elephant would throw back its trunk and blow its contents into your face. However, perhaps even that was preferable to the camel, who, baring its yellow teeth and spitting, would never miss if you were foolish enough to get too close. At the turning point of the ride was a small field and here en route you could stop and enjoy the antics of the chimps' tea party. Dressed in shirts and trousers, and little dresses, they would delight and enchant you with their table manners (scrambling all over them), and acrobatic skills. Then back to the starting point where the next group of passengers would be waiting.

Belle Vue was also famous for its zoo. Every animal, bird, fish and reptile on the planet I'm sure was housed there. Big cats, bears, camels, hippos, monkeys and apes, many species of snakes from huge pythons to small grass snakes, lizards and leopards were all kept in houses, and you could go from house to house to view all these exotic animals. Everyone was catered for according to their preference. If you cared to dance, the Elizabethan Room was a magnificent ballroom that hosted many championships and was also a Mecca for young people drawn from all over the North, and every weekend they would pack the dance floor to dance to the big bands of the era.

A terrifying spectacle was the wall of death. This was approached by a flight of steps leading to a platform that surrounded a huge drum construction. The riders would enter from a door at the base and mounting their bikes they would rev at full throttle and race around the vertical walls. Up and down, in and out, they would form intricate manoeuvres, narrowly missing one another and drawing gasps of admiration from the spectators viewing from above – sometimes screaming in horror as the riders shot to the rim of the drum almost becoming airborne.

To round off a great night you could witness a magnificent firework display. The historic battles, Waterloo, The Roundheads versus Cavaliers and many others were re-enacted with great authenticity, the costumes and weapons adding to the drama. The lake would double as the English Channel with boats full of invading soldiers, to be repelled by the defending army, shouting in victory and firing at the retreating enemy.

Greyhound racing and speedway racing all drew their enthusiasts, but for me the King's Hall reigned supreme. Apart from promoting wrestling every Wednesday and Saturday evening, some of the world's famous Championship Boxing matches were hosted there. Northern connoisseurs from around Manchester, Stockport, Liverpool, Bolton, Wigan, etc. still drool when they hear names such as Jackie Brown, Paddy Ryan, Johnny Cusick, Jack McAvoy, Johnny King, Alf Robinson, Bruce Woodcock, Henry Cooper, Brian London and many more who graced the ring at the King's Hall.

I have known boxers to fight on the booths on a Saturday afternoon and then top the bill at Belle Vue the same evening.

But there other great venues up and down the country: the Royal Albert Hall, Liverpool Stadium, Paisley Ice Rink (boy, was that cold – the ring was placed in the centre of the ice, and although a strip of carpet was provided, my bare feet were frozen by the time I reached the ring). Others that spring to mind are Nottingham Ice Rink, Leeds Town Hall, Granada Tooting, The Victoria Hall (Hanley, Stoke-on-Trent), and the smaller halls such as the Wryton Stadium Bolton – which spawned great wrestlers such as the Royal Brothers, Abe Ginsberg, Colin Joynson, Johnny Saint and many more.

On the seafront at Rhyl stood the Gaiety Theatre. The ring was placed directly on the stage floor which sloped quite steeply down towards the audience. If you were thrown up the ring you would travel in slow motion like the Bionic Man. Conversely if thrown down the ring you would travel like a bull at a gate.

I was on the bill with Honey Boy Zimba when his opponent threw him down the ring. With his legs gaining momentum by the second, Zimba failed to hook into the ropes and shot out of the ring like a rocket, dropping about 10 ft into the empty orchestra pit. Leaning over the ropes, the referee asked anxiously, 'Are you OK, Zimba? You haven't broken anything?' 'No, ref. There's nothing to break down here.' Always the joker, Zimba.

Hard men, great men

I recall a charity football match we played on the rugby ground in the middle of the speedway track at Belle Vue Stadium. We were playing the Show Biz Eleven captained by Tom Courtney. The charity was Cancer Research and Julie Goodyear sportingly kicked off for us. We had to borrow a ball from one of the shooting stands close by because the organisers had forgotten to bring one.

It was then I realised why I had never been able to score a goal at these stands. The ball was as heavy as a medicine ball. We looked like a team of pensioners as we hobbled off the pitch, leg muscles throbbing and feet aching. However, the ground was packed and the spectators enjoyed it, and most importantly we made a lot of money for Cancer Research.

Heroes and Villains

'Won't fit in your car? I'm only the size and weight of three ordinary men...'
Giant Haystacks

Why do professional wrestlers attract such an enormous viewing audience and pack the huge halls up and down the country, compared with amateur wrestling, judo contests and most other combat sports? It is not because they are fitter, more skilled or dedicated; it is because they are showmen. The hip throws, shoulder throws, suplexes, flying head mares, step-over leg locks, arm levers, full and half nelsons and Boston crabs, are used by professional and amateur alike, but the professionals will add showmanship, panache and flair.

Some adopt certain techniques to make them their own personal crowd puller; others enter the ring flamboyantly dressed and of course there are the rule benders, hated villains to the fans, but it is a love–hate relationship.

There were the masked men. The fans would flock to the venues where they were appearing in the hope that they would lose and therefore would have to unmask.

The tag teams were mostly made up of fabulous names who would join up with a colleague to form a wrestling duo with eye catching names such as: the Fabulous Royals – Bert and Vic Faulkner; the St Clairs – Roy and Tony St Clair; the Judokas – Al Marquette and Peter Roberts; the Silent Ones – Mike Eagen and Harry Kendall; the Black Diamonds – Abe Ginsberg and Eric Cutler; the Untouchables – Leon Arras and Lee Sharron; the Barons – Ian Gilmour and Jeff Kaye; the Bengal Tigers – Amarjit and Joga Singh; Hell's Angels – Adrian Street and Bobby Barnes; the Lincolnshire Poachers – Colin Joynson and Steve Haggerty; Mick McManus and Steve Logan; Jackie Pallo Senior and Jackie

Kent Walton: the man whose name became synonymous with professional wrestling.

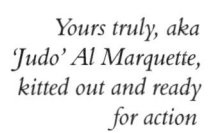

Yours truly, aka 'Judo' Al Marquette, kitted out and ready for action

Vic Hesselle,
one of the stars of The Blood Tub.

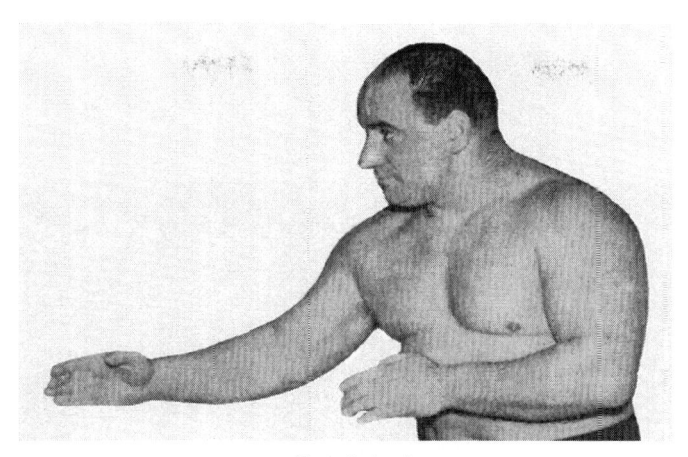

*Bert Assirati,
one of the stars of* The Blood Tub.

*Francis St Clair,
one of the stars of*
The Blood Tub.

Vic Hesselle training Bert Royal and Vic Faulkner at home.

Myself, Jimmy Saville, who had had a few bouts as a middleweight, the most notable against ex-world champion Gentleman Jim Lewis, and the huge Japanese heavyweight Shozo Kobayashi.

Alan Colbeck, my opponent on my first television appearance.

King's Hall poster.
Note the variation of the spelling of Vic's name and the fact that Tiger Woods was on the bill! Man Mountain Benny was the same Bill Benny in whose club in Levenshulme, Manchester I had my very first wrestling bout.

I have the 'Iron Man' Steve Logan in a half nelson and head twist at the Royal Albert Hall. Note that the Iron Man is no longer laughing at my 'pyjamas'.

Les Kellet tormenting Mick McManus.

Mike Marino was top of the bill at the first televised show in Novmber 1995.

Four PAGES OF UP-TO-THE-MINUTE NEWS & PICTURES

WRESTLING REVIEW

OFFICIAL PROGRAMME AND DETAILS OF TONIGHT'S CONTESTS AND CONTESTANTS

Volume III.   Edited by Charles "Spider" Mascall   Number 57

THIS WILL BE A ROYAL YEAR!

It is quite apparent to every enthusiastic wrestling follower that this will be a Royal Year in more ways than one.

The name of Bert Royal is on the tip of everyone's tongue. Back to wrestling arenas, this twenty-one year old red-robed welterweight from Bolton is bringing many supporters of his own making. In a weight class that boasts proudly of many crackerjack stars, Royal— by some very clever moves—is forcing his way into being not only the most popular welterweight in the land but most definitely the leading contender in the race for Jack Dempsey's crown.

In a month or two's time, Royal will go to Spain, where he will sojourn for the summer months. Also we understand from French sources that Royal will likely face the reigning European welterweight champion at the Palais des Sports before the current season is over.

Yes, it looks like being a Royal Year indeed.

Rene Ben Chemoul
who may come here
to meet
BERT ROYAL

THE OTHER SIDE OF CARLTON SMITH

Every Sunday Carlton Smith, far from the hustle-bustle of the ring, relaxes with his wife and boxer dog. Like any other normal husband the stormy little petrel of the wrestling ring is a typical family man. Rugged and fiery in the ring, as some of his rivals will confirm, Carlton likes nothing better than a quiet family life when he is home from his wrestling chores.

"BUDDY ROGERS" COMING TO EUROPE?

Off to the United States next week is French impresario Alex Goldstein, guiding hand behind many of the foremost wrestling stadiums in Europe. Whilst in New York Mr. Goldstein intends to make the most of his brief visit by combining business with pleasure. He hopes to sign Charles "Buddy" Rogers, New York's famous "Nature Boy" of wrestling, Marvin Mercer, Verne Gagne or Louis Thesz for contests in France and England.

Front cover of Wrestling Review *extolling the virtues of Bert Royal.*

Roy St Clair demonstrates the forearm smash. Roy followed in his father's footsteps into the licensed trade.

That's me on the right in 1963 after judging the Miss Cheshire Rose competition. Dominic Pye is on the left and the winner centre.

Count Bartelli practises his elephant throw.

Bob Francini was a hard man who won five regional titles. His first professional bout was against me at the King's Hall, Belle Vue, Manchester.

Tony St Clair is still wrestling in Germany and also runs a school for amateurs who hope to turn professional.

Wrestlers were in demand in the 1960s and 1970s. Here I am advertising yoghurt.

World Championship presentation in the ring.

All the wrestlers together.

Back row: Bob Sherry, the referee Lou Rosebury, Johnny Eagles, Jackie Robinson and Steve Haggerty.
Front row: Colin Joynson, Vic Faulkner, myself, Bobo Matu with the hotel's proprieter in a headlock, Abe Ginsberg, Paul Carpantier and Bert Royal.

Pallo Junior; Big Bruno and Alan Garfield; Tibor Szakacs and Steve Veidor; and many more names that must be engraved in the memories of their fans.

People, particularly the ladies, would scream abuse at the television screen when the likes of McManus, Pallo and Logan were appearing, but they would not miss a single minute of the hour between 4 and 5 p.m. on a Saturday afternoon. The bouts between McManus and Pallo, who always appeared on television before the Cup Final, were as popular as the football match itself. More so for the grannies who, after shouting themselves hoarse at the wrestlers, would then get up and make the family tea when the football came on.

Many of the wrestlers from around the Manchester, Wigan, Bolton and Liverpool areas were trained to Olympic standard with no frills or gimmicks. They knew their craft backwards and they were a joy to watch. All fans will recognise and remember great bouts, including names such as Johnny Saint, Ian Wilson, Peter Linberg, Bob Bell, Monty Swan, Marty Jones, Gypsy John Kenny, Alan Wood, Steve Wright and, of course, the Robinsons, the Royals, along with Colin Joynson, Steve Haggerty, 'Mr Universe' John Lees, and many others including Bobo Matu, a real hard mat man who, incidentally, can be spotted standing at the bar in the Rovers Return most evenings each week; he is an extra for Granada Television.

Another hard man was Bob Francini, an amateur who won five regional titles, making his professional debut at the Festival Hall, Brisbane, Australia. When he returned to the North of England in the late 1960s, his first professional bout was against me at the King's Hall, Belle Vue, Manchester. It was a hard, bruising, but thrilling bout and *The Wrestler* described it as 'the most exciting bout of the season'.

He was scientific and aggressive, plus a liberal use of knee, forearm and boot was employed, and a couple of weeks later we were billed together for a return match held in Sheffield. According to a local bylaw we had to be examined by a doctor before entering the ring. The police doctor, accompanied by a police sergeant, called your name from the programme and, entering a side room, you were given a quick check-up. Francini was called first and then I followed, stripped to the waist. The sergeant said, 'There must be some mistake – I want the Marquette who is fighting Francini.'

I said, 'I am Marquette and I am fighting Francini.'

Both the doctor and the sergeant eyed my very slim frame and the sergeant said to me, 'I never stay to watch the wrestling but I'm going to tonight – he must be 3 st. heavier than you.'

It was indeed a very hard-bruising bout, but I managed to win.

I wrestled Bob in a few more return bouts up and down the country and I rate him and Bert Royal among the very best mat men in the world.

Pete Linberg

Peter Lindop wrestled under the name of Pete Linberg. He was one of the strongest men in Britain. His build when dressed was very deceptive, looking not much different from the man in street, but when he was stripped for action the definition of his muscular physique was obvious.

He had appeared on *The David Frost Show* and if any reader happened to view that particular evening they would have been amazed to watch Pete bending 6 in. nails with his bare hands and tearing telephone directories in half. That was just one demonstration of his physical strength. His coup-de-grace was to blow up hot water bottles until they burst, a testament to his fantastic lung power. The first time I was billed against him was at a venue in Colne, Lancashire. As the bell rang for the first round I moved to the centre of the ring to make first contact with what is called the Referee's Hold. The left hand is placed behind your opponent's neck and your right hand grips his upper arm.

However, Linberg did not observe the niceties. He immediately claimed me and pressed me at arms length above his head with effortless ease. He walked towards the ropes and I had visions of being thrown about six rows back, breaking a few bones and injuring a few spectators. I groped for a handful of his hair but unfortunately he hadn't a lot to grab and luckily for me and the spectators he turned and slammed me down in the middle of the ring.

I found it virtually impossible to pin his shoulders for a fall or to apply a submission hold and by the middle of the fourth round I was tiring rapidly. He sensed this and stepped up the pressure, at one point throwing me so hard I shot through the ropes like a bullet, landing at the feet of the ringsiders. With the help of a few fans pushing me, I climbed back on to the apron. Linberg reached over the ropes hauled me back into the ring, body slammed me, then pinned my shoulders for a fall. As I returned to my corner I remember my second shaking his head and saying 'You don't stand a chance. This fellow's the strongest wrestler I've ever seen.'

In the fifth round I kept on the move and when I saw my chance I caught him in a hand tie – my speciality – and applied a sleeper hold. As he sank to the floor the ref counted him out. I then broke the hand tie and restored him to the land of the living. Linberg thought he'd been robbed, but the fans loved it. They like to see the underdog win.

I wrestled Pete a number of times in the early days, but because of contractual clauses, we did not meet in the ring again after 1968.

I was dismayed to learn he had suffered a heart attack after retiring. However, although it has slowed him down he is quite fit again and enjoys a chat about the old days.

Jackie (Mr TV) Pallo

Red-and-white, or blue-and-white striped trunks were the trademark of Jackie Pallo, along with his long blond curly locks tied at the back with a bow. He was a past master at aggravating both the crowd and his opponent; he must have been one of the most verbally abused wrestlers in the ring. He would strut around the ring arguing with the referee, adjusting the bow in his hair, re-tying his bootlaces, leaning over the ropes inciting the ringsiders, anything for effect that would leave his opponent standing in his corner looking like a lemon, waiting for the bout to begin. In fact he did more strutting around than wrestling, and pulling every dirty trick in the book to win.

I was billed against Pallo at the Victoria Hall, Hanley, Stoke-on-Trent and if stage performers claim that the Glasgow Empire was the toughest hall to succeed at, they should have tried the Victoria Hall at Hanley. It was a great Saturday night venue, but it was notorious for its women fans. Many of them worked at the pot banks, and, boy were they tough. They booked the same ringside seats every week, and woe betide any wrestler thrown out of the ring landing at their feet. Whether you were a hero or a villain, it made no difference, they got stuck into you kicking and swiping at you with their handbags. They were as much a part of the evening's entertainment as the wrestlers themselves. As a matter of fact, I think the fans enjoyed watching them as much as the wrestlers.

Sometimes they could get too carried away and often, for no apparent reason, would turn against a particular wrestler. Steve Haggerty, a hard man in the ring, was such a case. He told me that the women hated him and would be jeering and catcalling as his bout was taking place. As a matter of fact, it wasn't just Steve who came in for their abuse. His wife, Dorothy, often used to be spat upon.

The ring was erected ten feet from the stage, seating about forty spectators. At the corner of the stage was an easel with the following week's wrestling bill pinned to a piece of plywood about twenty-four by eighteen inches. Haggerty had thrown his opponent over the ropes and, each time he climbed back onto the ring apron, Haggerty kicked him off. A woman seated on the stage was so incensed that she snatched the board off the easel and skimmed it like a cigarette card. It his Haggerty on the back of the head, resulting in a cut needing seven stitches.

Stan Rylands, the referee, was a past master at calming things down, although the wrestlers seldom retaliated, accepting abuse from fans as an occupational hazard.

I remember one night watching a programme on television called *What's My Line?* Gilbert Harding, who had a short fuse at the best of times, was on the panel. The idea of the game was for contestants to mime their jobs and the panel to interpret their actions. A man came on and mimed holding something in his right hand and banging it with his left hand. The panel made a few guesses and then gave up. When asked what his job was, the man replied he was a 'sagger maker's bottom knocker' working in the pot banks. Gilbert Harding blew his top demanding to know how the panel could possibly interpret the actions of a job like that! I nearly fell off my chair laughing because it brought to mind my being thrown over the top ropes at the Victoria Hall and being kicked in the butt by the wife of a sagger maker's bottom knocker!

In the bout with Pallo, I had claimed him in a side head lock close to the ropes when suddenly this woman jumped to her feet and, swinging her handbag, caught him a blow to the side of his face, just as the bell sounded. I felt his knees sag, and I called the referee over and told him what she had done. Leaning over the ropes he asked her what she had in her bag. She opened it up and produced a pot of cold cream as big as a jar of marmalade, proudly holding it aloft for all to see. She must have deliberately brought it in to bash somebody with, and that just happened to be Jackie.

Another time I was against him at the Liverpool Stadium, another tough venue. It was always packed and the atmosphere was great. A woman threw a baby's dummy at Jackie and he casually kicked it towards his corner. He then threw me after it. I picked up the dummy and rammed it into his mouth. He stood there gobsmacked (literally!), and the fans exploded into laughter. I suppose I should not have done that since there was no knowing where it had been, but given the chance he would have done the same to me.

Later in the same bout yet another dummy, this time made of Blackpool rock, came hurtling into the ring, but this time it missed him and hit me on the nose. Strange the things that some women carry in their handbags.

For all Jackie's egoism and flamboyance in the ring, he was no slouch. He came from a fighting family, his father having been a well-known boxer, and Jackie followed in his footsteps before taking up wrestling.

We were sharing a dressing room at a venue, chatting as you do about nothing in particular, when he noticed in my bag were two blocks of wood measuring about 12 in. square and 2 in. thick. Curiosity overcoming him he asked me why they were in my bag, and I explained that the previous day I had been giving an exhibition of karate and aikido, and that I would break the wood either with my hands or my bare toes. Jackie challenged me to hold one up for him to break, taken aback when I replied 'You're having a laugh, you'll break your hand!' However, he insisted, and I held up the block for him to break, hardly able to keep the smirk off my face. I fully expected his hand to recoil, and to see him cursing in pain, but to my astonishment he broke the block of wood clean in half.

I can imagine him still gloating now.

Big Daddy

Towards the end of the seventies two big names burst into prominence on the wrestling scene and when I say big – I mean big. Between them they weighed in excess of 60 st.

Shirley Crabtree a.k.a. 'Big Daddy' and Martin Ruane a.k.a. 'Giant Haystacks' brought a new dimension to the game. Too huge to execute any of the holds requiring dexterity, nonetheless they were hugely popular as they butted with their stomachs and body slammed their opponents around the ring – finally falling on them full length in what they called the 'Big Splash', driving the very breath out of their opponents' bodies.

Shirley was born in November 1937 and according to my research his mother wanted a girl so badly she was determined to christen the baby Shirley, no matter whether it was a boy or a girl. He must have learnt how to fight at a very early age with a name like that.

By the time he reached his teens he was an excellent swimmer, a keen body builder and amateur wrestler. Both he and his two brothers, Max and Brian, became professional wrestlers while still in their teens, although only Shirley remained actively wrestling. Brian became one of the top television referees and Max became a senior director of Joint Promotions, wrestling's governing body. Shirley won two titles during the 1950s and 1960s and then he suddenly quit the game.

His brother Max became more powerful on the managerial and promoting side and in 1976 he persuaded Shirley to return to the ring, changing his name to Big Daddy after seeing the play *Cat on a Hot Tin Roof*. With top hat, Union Jack vest and short tights, Shirley became a huge hit with an estimated viewing audience of over 10 million, roughly one third of Britain's population. No one, including Hulk Hogan, The Rock or any other of the American wrestlers, has achieved this in their own country.

Giant Haystacks

A golfing friend of mine, Mike Earley, was the managing director of a food company near Haydock in Lancashire. He asked me if Big Daddy and I would judge a children's painting competition they were promoting. I rang Shirley, but unfortunately he was wrestling in London the same day and he suggested I approach Haystacks. I was rather reluctant as I had never met him and I wasn't sure that he would know me. He did however and agreed to judge.

Upon my arriving at his home to collect him, a young, pretty, petite lady answered the door. I introduced myself and she called her husband. The biggest man I have ever met in my life came to the door, 6 ft 11", and weighing 41 st. – I could not believe my eyes.

I thought, Oh, my poor car! – I had a Vauxhall Cavalier at the time and just about squeezed my long legs into it.

I said, 'I'm sorry but there is no way you will fit into my car'

'I'm only the size and weight of three ordinary men,' he replied.

'I know that,' I retorted, 'but they don't all sit on the same seat, they spread themselves around a bit.'

We had a good laugh about it and he agreed to follow me in his own car with its reinforced adaptable driving seat.

But what a lovely man he was. Quiet and well spoken, he made the children feel at ease and showed a keen interest in their work. He spent a lot of time posing for photographs with them and you could not believe he was the same man who became the scourge of the heavyweight division. He was a club bouncer before he realised he could make a good living wrestling and he wrestled all over Europe and America before his television debut in this country in 1975 when he teamed up with Big Daddy in a tag match against Roy and Tony St Clair. Why they did not stay together as tag partners I don't know, because I don't think any team in the world would have stood a cat in hell's chance against them, including the Americans. But it was not to be. For some reason they became hated, ferocious opponents.

Whenever they were matched against each other, unless you booked a seat well in advance it was standing room only. The promoters must have been rubbing their hands.

Because of Haystacks' huge size, television and film producers were very keen to have him on their books. I think his debut was in Brian Glover's TV play, *The Wild Bunch* followed by a part in Sir Paul McCartney's *Give My Regards to Broad Street*.

Recently I was at a celebrity golf reception at the Foyle Golf Club near Belfast, and had the pleasure of meeting the television personality Jackie Fullerton. He told me about the time he was conducting a television street interview with Giant Haystacks. Everything was fine until Jackie must have needled the Giant with a question about his doubting if they (the wrestlers) ever got hurt from some of the throws. Jackie invited him to demonstrate a throw, and without any further prompting Haystacks picked him up and body slammed him on to the pavement. Jackie told me he was really hurt and needed hospital treatment which proves my statement; that if you do not know how to break your fall, you can be seriously hurt.

However, because of the publicity and television repeats, Jackie is now quite a celebrity in Northern Ireland.

Haystacks spent a great deal of his career wrestling in Canada, America, New Zealand and Germany against the likes of Hulk Hogan and Andre the Giant. On returning to England the feud between him and Big Daddy, Kendo Nagasaki and Pat Roach would pack the halls to bursting point. The highlight of his career was winning the CWA World Heavyweight Championship.

In 1996 he took ill and was diagnosed with inoperable stomach cancer and died in November 1998. I attended his funeral along with his many friends from the world of wrestling.

A very sad loss to the wrestling world.

The Meanest Gunslinger in the North (West) and Other Crowd Pullers

'What the hell am I going to do without my bloody guns?'
Jack Cassidy

Jack Cassidy or, as he loved to be known, 'The English Cowboy', was larger than life both in size and personality. He was a firm favourite with the fans and, of course, the youngsters loved him.

He was a very striking and impressive figure in his Stetson hat, a kerchief tied around his neck, chaps and cowboy boots. In those days, western films were still being made – albeit spaghetti ones. Strapped around his hips rested two .45 revolvers and often promoters, anxious to advertise that evening's bout, would have him ride a horse around the town.

At nearly 6 ft in height and weighing 19 st. it required a very big horse and Jack was no Clint Eastwood. Sometimes he found them a bit hard to handle. He recalls late one Friday afternoon during peak traffic time, riding this huge horse through the Bull Ring, in Birmingham – an exercise even the Lone Ranger would have fought shy of. However, whether the horse was not used to traffic noise or lots of people milling around patting its hind quarters, it was impossible to say, but something must have spooked it because it suddenly took off at a full gallop. People leapt out of the way and, with Jack grimly hanging on, the horse eventually darted up a narrow passage behind Woolworths. Jack was well and truly stuck. Because of the size of the horse and the size of Jack, he could neither turn round nor dismount; they were both wedged.

Rescue came when someone pulled on the horse's tail until it slowly backed out whereupon it was promptly nipped on the leg by an overexcited Alsatian dog. Eyes bulging, it took off again, and Jack had visions of being carried off into the sunset like John Wayne, but control was gained and I have Jack's assurance that when he appeared at the venue that evening, after his experiences in the saddle, he was even walking like John Wayne!

His entrance into the ring was equally spectacular. On his head he wore a white Stetson, a lavishly decorated leather waistcoat, Cuban-heeled boots with spurs jangling, and with his six guns clunking, slung low ready for action, he made his way to the ring. As the referee introduced him, he would perform a fast draw and fire the guns into the air almost deafening the ringsiders.

One night Jack and I had been booked to appear at a big charity function so we had travelled down together in my car. Black tie and evening dress was the order of the day, and the good and great sat at tables surrounding the ring. As the MC announced him, Jack, as usual, aimed his guns into the air and fired, but unfortunately one of the metal plugs blocking the barrels shot out and blew a hole in the ceiling! Chunks of plaster showered down on to the ring floor, the tables and even the food on the plates, followed by a cloud of choking dust. The diners rose as one body and an undignified scramble ensued as they dived for cover. I suppose that is what you would call 'bringing the house down'!

We were on our way back up the M6 and Jack was asleep on the back seat when I saw the dreaded blue light flashing behind me. I was well within the speed limit and stone cold sober, so I was not unduly worried when I was pulled in. Jack was still dead to the world. Two police officers approached and I was asked to get out of the car and open the boot. Inside were our bags containing our wrestling gear. I explained that we were wrestlers returning from that evening's venue. They looked puzzled and one of them remarked, 'You should get your suspension checked mate; your bumper is nearly touching the road.' I inclined my head towards Jack still asleep on the back seat.

'Oh, that will be him. He weighs 19 st.,' I replied.

Now Jack always left the venues in his full cowboy gear including his guns. He did this because his fans would be waiting outside for his autograph and hopefully to have a photograph taken with him. You can imagine the policemen's faces when they looked into the car and saw Jack sprawled on the back seat, his guns still strapped around his waist. They nearly had a fit!

'Does he have a licence to carry those?' enquired one.

I shrugged my shoulders and said that I didn't know but the barrels were blocked and they only fired blanks.

'If he hasn't got permission from the Chief Constable's office, he's nicked,' he sniffed.

Jack was rudely awakened to find his guns being confiscated and grudgingly he unbuckled his belt and handed the guns over to the smirking boys in blue. He was not too pleased I can tell you; the air was punctuated with expletives!

We continued our journey with Jack fuming on the back seat of the car occasionally bewailing, 'What the hell am I going to do without my bloody guns?' He sounded like an old gunslinger from a Wild West film.

Needless to say they were returned to him, but only after he had acquired written permission. He was one of the great characters of the ring and, in spite of his size, he was very agile, a good wrestler and also very good fun.

Mick McManus

This name must evoke many memories of one of the best-known faces on British television during the heyday years. With his jet black hair trimmed to a point in the middle of his forehead, he became the symbol of a diabolical villain. Possibly Hitler was the most hated man of the last century – Mick must have run a very close second.

Although he stood about 5 ft 7", what he lacked in height he made up for in power and cunning. He could lift you clean off your feet with a forearm smash and he was not fussy where he hit you – in the kidneys, the throat, followed by grabbing a handful of hair and heaving you across the ring.

He would provoke the women spectators to a frenzy and as they screamed their abuse at him, he would pace the ring ignoring their taunts. One woman hurled her shoe into the ring at him. He calmly picked it up, broke it over his knee and threw it back to her. Those were the days.

He seldom lost a bout and I am very proud to be one of the few to claim a victory over him. I was matched against him in London, and Lew Marco, who was as famous as the wrestlers, was refereeing the match. Marco will be remembered for his style of lying on the ring floor or along the bottom rope to check that the shoulders were touching the canvas. His way of counting, 'one-ar, two-ar', would be echoed by the crowd. This particular night he was lying, his face very close as I was trying to pin McManus.

Mick brought his knee up into the pit of my stomach causing me to cough, and unintentionally I spat into Marco's face. This prompted Lew to cease the count and utter in disgust, 'You dir'y norven 'eaven, you spit right in my boat race!' This translated from Cockney slang means, 'You dirty northern heathen, you have spat right in my face!'

I claimed McManus, threw him into the corner post and aimed a chop at his head. He ducked, and I hit the iron stanchion breaking my little finger. That cost me the bout.

I last saw Mick at the last wrestlers' reunion in Kent in August 2007. He still has the same hairstyle and does not look a day older than the last time we met in the ring. Happily, our meeting this time was a lot friendlier.

Billy Two Rivers

What can be said about this man? A great deal. Billy was one of the most charismatic wrestlers that ever graced the ring in this country and I came to know him well.

Many times we were on the same bill and I would pick up Billy from the place he was staying to drive him to the venues. Normally he was dressed in a suede buckskin jacket with fringes across the chest and down the sleeves. This was tame stuff to what he wore in the ring.

With the spotlights full upon him, he emerged from the dressing room wearing a fully feathered Mohican Indian head-dress and upon its removal displayed a Mohican hairstyle which, incidentally, became a fashion trend among the youths of the day.

What an awesome sight he portrayed; nothing like this had ever been seen on British television before and he became an instant hit with the fans, including my wife, Pat, who has admitted to me that before we met she would go to watch Billy, but never once did she see me!

He was a clever and stylish wrestler but if provoked he would perform a buck and wing war dance and an Indian chant, so that everyone knew what was coming – invariably a tomahawk chop to the throat which usually ended the bout, whereupon he donned his headdress again and danced in victory around the ring. Everyone in the place would stand and cheer him, stamping their feet in unison (including my wife, Pat).

A full-blooded Mohawk Indian, Billy was born in 1935 on the Kahnawake Reservation near Montreal, Canada. I know very little of how he actually started, but in 1950 a wrestling superstar named Don Eagle returned home to the Kahnawake Reservation to recover from injuries sustained in the ring. They became good friends and when Eagle was ready to return, he persuaded Two Rivers to go with him, although at the time he was only fifteen years old.

They went to Columbus, Ohio, where Billy was trained for two years by Don Eagle and, in February 1953, he made his debut as a junior heavyweight in Detroit. As he became more experienced, he formed a tag team with his mentor which lasted from 1955 to 1959.

It was suggested to him that he should go to England, but the Calgary and Stampede tournaments were on at the same time, so he tossed a coin and, thankfully, England won. He was an overnight sensation, returning many times to the delight of his legion of fans.

When in England he would stay at a friend's pub in Heaton Moor, Stockport, and it was from there that I would pick him up if we were on the same bill, which was quite often, and drive him to the venue. We had many interesting conversations on those journeys and Billy would tell me about his life on the reservation and its limitations. When we hear the word 'reservation' it conjures up impressions of tepees and camp fires on the plains of America, just like the old Hollywood films. But far from it. The reservation consisted of high-rise flats very much like our own. Work was hard to come by and most of the young men worked as spidermen, erecting the girder frames for the skyscrapers.

Alcohol was forbidden, and he liked a drink or two in those days, did Billy! Many times on our way back from a venue we would stop at a pub just in time for last orders, but he was so popular I had my work cut out prising him away before midnight.

We were on our way back after a venue in the Midlands and Honey Boy Zimba was also with us. We pulled up at the first pub we saw because, as usual, it was almost closing time. The landlord welcomed us with open arms when he recognised who we were, particularly Billy, and invited us to stay after last orders. The drinks flowed but I was driving as usual, so I had to watch as Billy and Honey Boy were getting merrier by the minute. Then, from under the counter the landlord produced a bottle of wine and handed it to Billy. It was a very expensive bottle and I am sure it was the landlord's intention for Billy to take it home to enjoy. Instead Two Rivers asked for a bottle opener and he and Zimba glugged it down.

For all they cared it could have been firewater! Zimba's eyes began to glaze over but he manfully struggled on to put away a few more.

I managed, with great effort, to get them both back into the car. Zimba was almost out for the count and I threatened to throw them out if either of them dared to be sick in my car. When we eventually arrived back in Manchester, I offered to drop Billy off first, but to my amazement he insisted that I dropped them both at this club that he knew. Two Rivers hauled a semi-comatose Zimba off the back seat and, holding one another up, they staggered down the steps ready for the next session. I left them both there and drove home wondering how on earth they would manage to squeeze another drop down their throats, but they did.

During the interval at the Floral Hall, Southport, Billy and I were talking in the dressing room when Karl Denver of the Karl Denver Trio walked in. He was appearing in a nightclub, and seeing our names on the wrestling posters, called in to invite us back to the club after the bouts for a couple of drinks. Not wanting to appear a party pooper I agreed but with reservations because the following night we were both on the same bill again at Wolverhampton and I knew from experience that I would have a struggle to get Billy home.

It was after midnight before the show finished and a couple of drinks later I suggested we head back to Stockport, but Billy was in the mood now and was reluctant to go. So Karl persuaded me to leave Billy, promising me that he would personally take him home later. I agreed.

At four o'clock the next day I arrived to collect him as arranged, only to be told by his landlady that he had not come back the night before. He did not turn up at the Wolverhampton venue either. As a matter of fact it was several days before I saw him again. Enquiring where he had been, he looked me straight in the eye and said, 'Don't ask, Al, don't ask.'

Chatting to Steve Haggerty one night, Billy Two Rivers' name cropped up in our conversation. At that time Steve and his wife, Dot, owned a cracking little pub in Stockport and he told me that on their way back from a venue he had invited Billy back for a drink or two. Time passed very quickly and, since it was late, Steve invited him to stay the night. That one night stretched to a month and Steve said he had never seen so many gin and tonics drunk in all his years in the business!

After returning to Canada he continued to wrestle for a further six more years, finally retiring in 1978.

For the following twenty years he sat on a council leading the Mohawks of the Kahnawake reservation. With his wealth of experience travelling the world, he soon became the External Affairs Minister, and is now the Senior Policy and Political Advisor to the Assembly of First Nations. He is a national figure, proud of his heritage, and, in spite of his success and fame, he has never lost touch with his roots, and remains to this day a modest and unassuming man.

Ricky Starr

Another great wrestler from across the water was Ricky Starr. Arriving in England in the sixties, he had trained as a ballet dancer in his native New York.

He was a contradiction in terms; although he had the build of a ballet dancer with all the natural grace and muscular definition, he was also a very competent and stylish wrestler. He was immensely fit and acrobatic, performing, without effort, back somersaults to escape the locks and holds.

He would frustrate his opponents with his athleticism and his ability to make them look awkward and clumsy. As the bell sounded his opponent would come to the centre of the ring ready to claim him. He would perform an arabesque and then, pirouetting around the ring he would cheekily smack their bottoms as he danced by. The fans thought this hilarious but his opponents did not, especially Steve Logan. Incensed, he would charge across the ring coming off the worst every time. Unlike many other wrestlers whose appearance would be their trademark, Ricky Starr had no such gimmicks. Spurning even a robe, he just wore trunks and incredibly instead of wrestling boots on his feet he wore ballet shoes.

Out of the ring he was a reserved and private man of few words, very likeable and well respected by fans and wrestlers alike. Although I never met him in the ring, I feel that I cannot miss the opportunity to record the skills and entertainment value of such an exceptional talent.

Andy Robin and Hercules

Hercules stood about 3 ft in height when he first appeared in the ring, and at the end of his illustrious career towered to almost 7 ft. He was covered with hair, had a great sense of fun and loved to be patted and tickled back in his dressing room. He starred in films, television adverts and made many personal appearances throughout his life. The crowds loved him, we loved him and so did his owner, Andy Robin. Hercules was a cuddly bear cub, and Robin would bring him into the ring for a few moments and playfully wrestle him around it.

The crowd loved it and I'm certain so did Hercules, but after he was returned to the dressing room, what remained in the ring was the hardest, most uncompromising wrestler ever to come out of Scotland. His strength was phenomenal: he would roll a huge cartwheel down and into the ring, and before the bout began he would press the wheel above his head, and lowering it to the floor would then invite his opponent or any member of the crowd to 'have a go'. A few tried, but I don't think anyone succeeded; that was until the Japanese wrestler Shozo Kobayashi was matched against him at the Drill Hall, Dumfries.

Accepting the challenge Kobayashi pressed the wheel but, instead of lowering it, he dropped it to the floor where it went straight through, splitting the boards and ripping the canvas. The floor of the ring was made up of a metal frame with 6 ft by 3 ft panels dropped into place and covered with a canvas sheet. The stewards replaced the broken panel with a folding table from the canteen, the measurements being roughly the same. Pulling the canvas together they stuck it with adhesive tape; the idea was good but unfortunately the table was thicker than the broken panel. The rings were hard enough to fall on at the best of times, without the addition of a ridge to land on. The promoter, Jack Atherton, was furious and I wasn't too pleased either, since my bout followed and, as I always wrestled in my bare feet I received a few very painful stubbed toes.

Andy Robin also formed the Eldorado All Stars team along with some other of Scotland's hard men, namely John Scot, Lee Thomas, Jim McKenzie, Mick McMichael and Ian Gilmour, taking on six-man teams from all over Britain. He captained the All Stars and went on to skipper a three-man team to compete in the promoter Max Crabtree's 'Battle Royal' competitions.

As for Hercules, he lived out his life in a special unit built for him, attached to the home of Andy Robin, where he died of old age in the year 2000.

The Original Undertaker

The well-known saying, ships that pass in the night, can also be the case with wrestling. Sometimes you are matched with someone that you will never meet in the ring again.

My bout with the Undertaker was such an encounter. It had been arranged at a Manchester night club and, as usual, I arrived not knowing whom I would be matched against. A hearse parked outside the entrance to the dressing rooms caught my attention.

'Who's died?' I asked the promoter.

'Nobody yet,' he answered me, 'but you are on against the Undertaker tonight, so watch out it's not you they carry back to the dressing room in a coffin.'

Without thinking, I retorted, 'Over my dead body.'

The lights were dimmed and the 'Dead March' droned mournfully through the loudspeakers. Two young men dressed in black slowly carried a coffin down the aisle and placed it on a bier next to the ring. A sombre silence descended. The undertaker slowly followed them, dressed in a black frock coat and a black silk top hat with black ribbons hanging down the back.

I was following him and, as I stepped into the ring, his two assistants came over to my corner and began to measure me up. I told them to bugger off and measure him up, because it would be him who would be leaving in the coffin.

The crowd had certainly been captured by the mood and I felt a surge of sympathy for me from the fans who must have thought I was about to meet my maker. What they did not know was that I too had a speciality of my own – a Japanese hand tie. Folding my opponent's hands and elbows, I would lock them together so it was virtually impossible for them to escape, until I was ready to release them. I would tip them over for a shoulder press or I would apply pressure to the main arteries which would put them to sleep long enough to be counted out. I would then revive them with a technique called Katsu, which would speed up the flow of blood to the brain.

During the bout, whenever I hyped the Undertaker over, his assistants would jump into the ring and try to pull me off him. They certainly knew how to take a bump because I kicked them through the ropes a couple of times.

In the third and fourth rounds he tried very hard to get his sleeper hold on me but I had had too much experience during my judo days countering that very hold. I think he realised that he did not have a chance of winning the bout unless he changed his tactics, so he settled down to more conventional wrestling. In the fifth round I tied his hands and applied my sleeper hold and he went out like a light. I indicated to his assistants to put him the coffin.

They were reluctant at first until I threatened to put them both in with him. I released the hand lock and ensured that he was recovering; they then carried him back to the dressing room.

The fans loved it and it was another victory for me, but, as I have already said, we never met in the ring again. He had a great, unique style and there have been a few 'undertakers' since in the wrestling rings, but none captured the crowds as he did.

Gentleman Jim Lewis

Standing just under 6 ft, of medium build and fairish hair, he cut an attractive figure in the ring. How Jimmy Lewis ever got the title of gentleman I shall never know, for there was nothing gentle about him.

He was one of the 'old school' of wrestlers; he knew every trick in the book and he used every one of them including a good helping of fist, knee and elbow. Jimmy Saville can vouch for that. I'll bet he still bears the scars from his encounter with him, I know I do.

On one occasion, Jimmy Lewis was driving Peter Linberg and me to Boston in Lincolnshire, and we were all on the same bill. The weather was atrocious, the rain was pouring down and the visibility was poor. Then the windscreen wiper packed up. This was in the days before the network of motorways that we have nowadays. Traffic was light that afternoon and we were able to travel on, however, very carefully. Jimmy then remembered that someone had told him that a cow heel wiped over the windscreen would allow the rain to glide off. At the very next town he found a butcher and a cow heel. I think that it should have been just a small piece that was needed, but Jimmy rubbed on the whole thing. The rain did run off but we still couldn't see through the windscreen for cow heel and Jimmy had to drive with his head out of the window. Peter and I were helpless with laughter.

It was still raining hard on our way back when Jimmy spotted a little garage and petrol station. Hoping that we might get some sort of repair we pulled in. It was closed. Jimmy said he would knock on the door to try to get some sort of help. Peter and I were not too sure but it was dark and late. He banged on the door and a light came on upstairs. A moment later the door opened and a huge man stood there. We expected a blast of ripe language from him but he said, 'As I live and breathe, it's Jimmy Lewis.'

We were ushered into the kitchen and he made coffee for us explaining that he was a retired policeman and had often been on duty at Belle Vue wrestling. What a relief it was. He repaired the wiper and we arrived back late but intact.

A few weeks later I was billed against Jimmy Lewis in Belfast. The referee was a young Irish lad and it was the first time he had officiated at a major wrestling tournament. Jimmy Lewis knew no other way to wrestle, only fast and furious from the first bell, so you had to be quick on your feet and so did the referee. Unfortunately this young lad was not and he was knocked off his feet a few times by either Lewis or me, as we were thrown across the ring.

He told me later in the dressing room that his ambition had always been to become a professional wrestler but now he was not so sure after experiencing the likes of Jimmy Lewis.

Kings, Queens and a Black Comedy

'Wrestled him? He's never wrestled anyone in his life, but there's a wrestler being buried on the other side of the cemetery.'
Funeral mourner

George Kidd

Many wrestlers were famous in many different ways. A spectacular hold or throw, the flamboyant gear they wore in the ring, a mask, their gigantic size or physique, each might distinguish them.

One man, however, was so skilful, agile and such a superb wrestler, he did not need any of those pegs to hang his ring image on. He was the most scientific wrestler that I had ever seen. Although slight of build, standing 5 ft 6" and weighing 11 st. he was for many years the undisputed lightweight champion of the world. His name was George Kidd.

As he was an expert escapologist his capability to extricate himself from most holds would make his opponents appear clumsy in comparison. I have wrestled George Kidd twice and came off second best on both occasions. Many of the moves and holds he had personalised to make his own. For example, when thrown and hitting the canvas he would instantly draw his knees up to his chest and lock his arms around them, making it impossible for any attempt at a shoulder press. If his opponent persisted he would roll around the ring like a ball until the guy gave up in frustration.

Another of his moves that was certain to thrill his fans was his version of the leg scissors, combined with a body swing, on many occasions gaining him a submission. Yet another move unique to him was one whereby, while standing, he would raise his leg waist high, inviting his opponent to grip his foot or ankle. This done, he would leap in the air, falling to the canvas on his back, at the same time locking their grip with his other foot, and with a spin of his hips he would send them flying across the ring.

The first time I was billed against him was at the Drill Hall, Dumfries. We were topping the bill but on arrival the promoter, Jack Atherton, told me that George was snowbound in Dundee and a substitute had been arranged at short notice; and a rematch would be held at his next promotion in a fortnight's time.

A couple of days before, Jack rang me to say that the roads were still blocked and the bout was postponed. I was very disappointed. Later the same week I was sharing a dressing room with Abe Ginsberg.

He said to me, 'Are you tired of living Marquette?'

'Why do you ask that?' I inquired.

Abe passed to me a leaflet he had picked up in Dumfries – they had been handed out to the fans. It read:

The reason George Kidd is not appearing is not because of the snow but because he is scared to death of me and he knows he would not stand a chance.

Al Marquette

The promoters had orchestrated the whole thing to maximise bums on seats. As you can imagine, when I eventually arrived at the Drill Hall it was packed to capacity.

During my journey to Dumfries I had been working out in my mind how I would counter George's moves. I had always made a point of watching George's bout if I was on the same bill, because he was always developing some new variation of his extensive range of throws and escapes.

'How naive can you get?' I thought.

As I climbed into the ring I was not expecting the reception that awaited me. For the first time in my career, boos and catcalls greeted me. These changed to cheers and applause as George walked down the aisle to the ring. I thought I bet he can't wait to screw my head off but he climbed through the ropes, came over to me, shook hands and wished me a safe bout.

I thoroughly enjoyed our first encounter, with us both

I take on Leon Arras aka Brian Glover. Brian was also a schoolteacher who made a second career in acting, starting with a memorable role in the hit film Kes.

Mick McManus has his opponent in a headlock. Mick must have run Hitler close as the most hated man of the twentieth century!

I am in control during a bout with Jackie 'Mr TV' Pallo. Jackie was a past master at aggravating both the crowd and his opponent.

Pat Roach was another wrestler turned actor, landing a great role in the hit series Auf Wiedersehen, Pet. *Sadly, Pat passed away in the summer of 2004.*

Les Kellet finds a suitable opponent. His partnership with Joe Critchley produced one of the funniest tag teams in the game.

Vic Royal comes over the ropes to help brother Bert. They were without doubt the most popular tag wrestling team in Europe. Note the poor referee at the bottom of the pile.

George Kidd was the most scientific wrestler that I had ever seen and was for many years the undisputed lightweight champion of the world.

Ricky Starr came to the UK from America. Arriving in England in the sixties, he had trained as a ballet dancer in New York.

Steve Haggerty with a headlock on Tony St Clair. Steve partnered Colin Joynson in tag wrestling.

Andy Robin owned Hercules, a cuddly bear cub, whom he would bring into the ring for a few moments and playfully wrestle.

Dressed to thrill: Adrian Street was born in Brynmawr, near Cardiff, but left to make a name for himself in London in the early sixties.

Abe Ginsberg, who began his career as a boxer, was part of the Black Diamonds tag team.

Billy Two Rivers was one of the most charismatic wrestlers that ever graced the ring in this country.

*Quasimodo was a French wrestler who turned a cruel quirk of
nature into a great success.*

Kendo Nagasaki was the most famous of all masked men. He never revealed his true identity during his career.

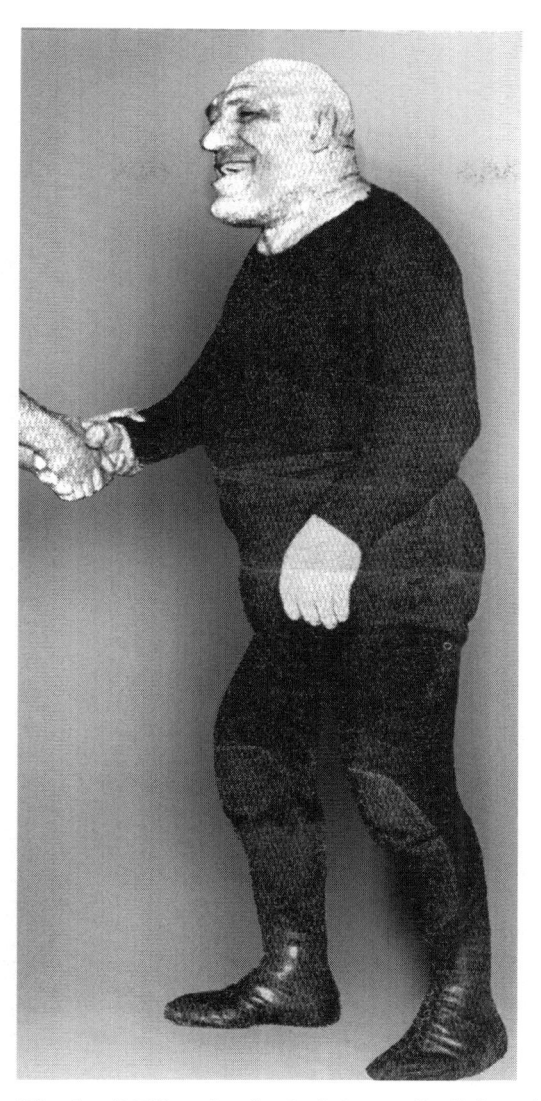

Maurice 'The Angel' Tillet who, despite being cruelly disfigured, was a reputable rugby player who played for his native France between 1926 and 1929.

Hell's Angels: Adrian Street and Bobby Barnes.
They were the campest wrestling act on the circuit. Bobby soon built up a huge following of female fans with his good looks and physique.

George Bollas – better known as The Zebra Kid. You wouldn't want to cross him! He was just under six feet in height and weighed over twenty-four stone but, in spite of his bulk, he was remarkably fast on his feet.

I had been wrestling for about six months for Joint Promotions when I first met Steve Logan.

Julien Morice was another of the French invaders. To help pay for his studies in medicine, he joined a wrestling club and within three years he had won both French and European lightweight championships. He then decided to concentrate his energies in the wrestling ring full time.

The Fabulous Royals, who endeared themselves to the fans by giving as good as they got.

Billy Robinson was the nephew of the great Alf Robinson. Alf fought and beat all comers on his way to the top in the boxing ring, defeating Norman Baines to win the Lonsdale Trophy at the Wembley Arena in 1937.

Me and Giant Haystacks. Martin Ruane, alias Giant Haystacks, along with Big Daddy (Shirley Crabtree) brought a new dimension to the game. Too huge to execute any of the holds requiring dexterity, they were nonetheless hugely popular as they butted their way with their stomachs and body-slammed their opponents around the ring, finally falling on them full length in what they called the 'Big Splash' – driving the very breath out of their opponents' bodies.
By the way, that's me on the right!

appreciating each other's moves and counters, and although I gained the first fall I lost the bout by two falls to one. At least I had redeemed myself in the eyes of the fans.

We talked afterwards and George told me that he had not even been booked for the first two bouts, nor had he seen the leaflets.

He retired undefeated Lightweight Champion of the World in the late seventies having built up successful businesses in hotels and petrol stations. He also fronted his own weekly television show on Grampian TV and was voted Television Personality of the Year in 1965.

Sadly no longer with us he was a legend in his own lifetime. There will never be another George Kidd.

The Danger Men – Colin Joynson and Steve Haggerty

Steve Haggerty and Colin Joynson, aka 'The Danger Men', certainly lived up to their title. Clad in black leotards with a skull and crossbones emblazoned on the front, muscles rippling from their necks, shoulders, arms and thighs, this pair were an awesome duo.

Formed in 1968, they wrestled all over Europe during the seventies, beating the cream of the continental tag teams in the process. Back in Britain, they soon became famous names with their many television performances and I think I'm right in saying they were the only tag team to beat the Fabulous Royals in a televised bout from Fleetwood, Lancashire.

Born in London in 1937, Steve turned professional in the mid-fifties. After more than twenty years in the ring, he retired and ran a pub with his wife, Dot. Today, Steve suffers with his knees from all the knocks and bumps they took during his career, but generally he's in good health and I don't think the many fans that followed him would have difficulty recognising him.

When his tag partner, Colin, retired, he and his wife also decided to run a pub, this time in the Manchester area. In 2003, after many years of problems with his right leg, he was forced to have it amputated just below the knee. What a courageous attitude he adopted afterwards – I'd have made more fuss over losing a tooth that Colin did over losing part of his leg! He and his wife Helen have carried on their lives as normal and this year, on our annual trip to Kent for the Wrestlers' Reunion, Colin and Helen were the life and soul of the journey.

After meeting many of the lads once again, we began our journey back home and, during a stop at a service station, Colin got his let trapped in the sliding door but obviously had not felt it. This prompted him to recount a story about a time he and Helen went for a meal to an Indian restaurant. On returning to their car, he was putting his false leg in when the wind blew the door shut. He was about to pull away, when he yelled, 'Where's my bloody leg?' Looking out of the window, he could see it lying in the car park. Helen thought it was hilarious and couldn't stop laughing as they attempted to shove it back up his trouser leg.

As well as his 'everyday' leg, he also had a swimming leg. This is punctured with many small holes, which allow water to seep in so it weighs roughly the same as his other leg, thus maintaining his balance. A very well-conceived idea, except Colin told me of the time he was on holiday and, coming out of the sea, the water flowed out of his leg like a colander. More embarrassing still, as he walked back up the beach there was an awful squelching sound that made it seem he was breaking wind with every stop. As a footnote, pardon the pun, Colin and Helen gave me permission to recount these stories, providing further testament to their sense of humour and attitude of making the best of whatever life dished in their direction.

The Fabulous Royals

Tag wrestling[1] was one of the most popular and exciting contests, both on television and around the venues; and of all the great teams already mentioned, I think all of us would agree that the most popular team in Europe was the Royal brothers, Bert and Vic.

What endeared them to the fans was the fact that they gave as good as they got. If both their opponents were in the ring attacking one of them, the other would not stand on the apron

---

[1] See Tag wrestling rules, p.88.

whingeing to the referee. He would be over the ropes, body slamming them, and then a favourite move of theirs would be to both squat down, claim their opponents' ankles and row them like a boat – very painful.

Most wrestlers, when tagged, would enter the ring using their own skills and techniques but Bert and Vic always worked as a team, using combinations and unusual holds they had perfected in the gym. As one tagged the other jumped in and carried on where the other had left off, so they got no respite. One of Bert's techniques was a wrist snap. He would throw you with an arm whip and then snap your wrist back. It felt like an electric shock ripping up your arm.

It was an education to watch them running rings around their opponents unless you were on the receiving end, as indeed I was at the Tower, Blackpool.

Pete and I had been matched against them and, as usual, it was a packed house. At one stage during the bout, Bert kicked me so high with a monkey climb that I shot up into the air, feet first, and shattered the ring lights. The bout had to be suspended until all the broken glass had been swept from the ring. Because of the height, it was difficult to time my breakfall and I came down on the back of my neck. I thought I'd broken it.

In the dressing room, after the bout, a few names were muttered under my breath and 'Fabulous' was not one of them.

However, all these incidents in the ring are forgiven and forgotten and when we meet up there is no animosity. We have a laugh and drink to the old days.

The Black Knights

Honey Boy Zimba and Jumping Jim Moser made up the tag team named the Black Knights. They both lived in Manchester and would pack the venues up and down the country, particularly the King's Hall, Belle Vue.

Jim Moser was also a talented footballer, turning out for the Northern Television Wrestlers team most weekends. After Honey Boy Zimba hung up his boots, he became a Manchester publican, and in 1999 he sadly died. Most of the northern wrestlers attended his funeral and Colin Joynson and Hans Streiger arranged to meet at the cemetery gates. The cortege arrived and a jazz band led the mourners through the cemetery.

Colin and Hans followed behind and, after the burial, one of the mourners recognised them and came over to ask them how they knew the deceased. Colin answered that they had wrestled him a few times over the years and were paying their respects.

'Wrestled him?' replied the mourner. 'He's never wrestled anyone in his life, but there's a wrestler being buried on the other side of the cemetery!'

They had followed the wrong funeral.

Les Kellet and Joe Critchley

One of the funniest tag teams in the game was Les Kellet and Joe Critchley. Their antics and clowning around kept the fans in hysterics. You could always guarantee a packed house whenever Les and Joe appeared – they were so popular.

Nevertheless, for all their amusing antics, they were both very good wrestlers. Nobody took liberties with those two.

Pete and I were billed against them at the Wryton Stadium in Bolton, Lancashire. Les came into the ring first, followed by Joe dressed as usual in a gaudy dressing gown, and carrying a trug basket full of flowers which he then began to throw to the ladies.

I was facing Les at the start of the first round and after a few minutes he turned to tag Joe, but he had disappeared off the apron. Pete and I must have tagged at least a couple of times and poor Les was beginning to flag. Eventually Joe rolled up and climbed back on to the ring apron. Les held up his hands and shouted, 'Stop, lads!' bringing the bout to a halt. Then, to Joe, he demanded, 'Where the bloody hell have you been?'

'I've been for a pee,' Joe answered, and the fans erupted. They loved the banter between them.

We, of course, would play up to them. One of Les's favourite moves was to fall back through the ropes, catching the bottom rope with his feet. He would spring back and hit his opponent with a forearm smash. I am sure everyone who ever watched Les wrestle will remember that move.

Certain procedures had to be observed before a bout started. The referee would inspect each wrestler by examining his hands and nails then, turning him around, he would run his hands over the back to determine any evidence of grease that may have been applied. Finally, his boots would be checked for any sharp objects. The referee would tap the back of the leg and the foot would be raised.

At one hall in the Midlands when the referee tapped Kellet's leg, instead of just raising it as usual, he swung his leg backwards, knocking the referee clean over the ropes. The crowd may have found it funny, but the referee certainly did not.

Adrian Street and Bobby Barnes – Hell's Angels

One of the biggest impacts on the world of tag wrestling was the launch of the Hell's Angels; Adrian Street and Bobby Barnes.

As they minced down the aisle from the dressing room to the ring in matching dressing gowns of shimmering gold fabric, it was hard to imagine them as Hell's Angels covered in sequins with high-standing collars. The robes flowed down to their gold and silver trimmed boots.

They would make a big show of taking each other's gowns off, folding them very carefully and handing them to their second to be taken immediately to their dressing room. A necessary precaution. They would have disappeared for souvenirs if left ringside.

Underneath they wore colourful trunks and elaborately patterned waistcoats. Tanned and fit, they had well-muscled bodies. Long blond hair flowed down to their shoulders as they pranced around the ring, deliberately camping it up to the delight of the ladies and the catcalls from the men.

Many of their opponents thought they were a couple of pansies and could be easily seen off, but they soon found to their cost it was only a front. They were very hard men indeed. They both had a sound grounding in the amateur ranks of both boxing and wrestling before turning pro, and in fact Adrian Street travelled around the fairgrounds with a boxing booth taking on all comers, not only to make a few bob, but also to gain experience. They both built up reputations in single bouts before joining up as a tag team.

Bobby Barnes was born in Lewisham, South London and soon earned a huge following of female fans with his good looks and physique. He had two tremendous encounters with Jackie Pallo. The second was a five ten-minute round bout at Beckenham Baths for the Bob Hunter Silver Cup. In round two, Bobby gained the first fall with a suplex followed by a shoulder press. Pallo equalised with a fall in round three.

In round four they were in a clinch, each trying to gain advantage when they both toppled through the ropes and landed in the ringside seats with Bobby's left leg taking the brunt of the impact. He was helped back into the ring by a couple of fans, but Pallo instantly tipped him over, put pressure on the injured leg and gained a submission, winning him the bout and the trophy.

Although it was described as the most exciting bout of the season, Bobby was very disappointed and so was his wife Brenda, who was watching the bout from the opposite side of the ring to Trixe Pallo – Jackie's wife. Brenda insisted that without the injury Bobby would have won the trophy.

Adrian Street was born in Brynmawr, near Cardiff, but left to make a name for himself in London in the early sixties. With his impressive physique he was in big demand as a model for artists and photographers but his ambition was to become a professional wrestler. He trained hard and was finally spotted by promoter Jack Dale and offered a contract with Joint Promotion. Within two years he beat Johnnie Williams to take the Welsh Lightweight Championship. After winning the title he was brimming over with confidence and this began to reflect in his arrogant style and dress.

I wrestled Adrian both in single bouts and tag matches. In one particular bout at Derby Baths he wound up the fans more than usual with his antics. As he left the ring an irate fan ran over, called him all the names under the sun, including an arrogant bastard, and then lashed out at him with his raincoat. Streety snatched the coat off him and strode to the dressing room, pushing the man aside. He then tore the lining out of it and plunged the lot into a tub of water.

Shortly afterwards the promoter entered asking for the return of the raincoat. Streety pulled it out of the tub and, handing it over, said if there were any complaints the man could wait outside for him. Needless to say the man and his sodden raincoat had vanished.

In the early nineties Adrian emigrated to the USA where I believe that he now has a prosperous business supplying all the fancy gear, belts and props to American wrestlers.

The Black Diamonds

The Black Diamonds tag team was formed by Abe Ginsberg and his first partner was a wrestler from Yorkshire who went by the name of John Fole. I regret I do not know much about him, except that he emigrated to America in the 1980s and apparently died there. Abe then found a new partner, Eric Cutler, from Eckington, Derbyshire, and together they toured the halls, both in this country and on the Continent.

Abe began his career as a boxer, learning the hard way by taking on all comers on the fairground booths. He began his wrestling career in the early 1960s, the boom time for wrestling that lasted up to the mid-1980s. His tag team's trademark was their gear which consisted of black tights, black vests and black leather helmets. Pete Roberts and I had some hard tussles with them and they had some great bouts with the Royal Brothers and Roy and Tony St Clair.

Abe told me this story of the days they wrestled on the Continent and they had been booked to fight in a small town on the border of Germany and Holland. The German MC, a small, immaculately dressed man sporting a grey Van Dyke beard and bristling with importance, came to the dressing room for details of Abe's and Eric's backgrounds. He asked Abe first, 'Vere do you come vrom?'

Abe answered, 'Manchester, England.' The MC looked puzzled and it was obvious that he had never heard of such a place.

Turning to Eric, he repeated the question, 'Und vere are you vrom?'

'Eckington,' replied Eric. The MC's face lit up. 'Ah, Eckington in Derbyshire. Vunderbar, I know it well!'

Abe never found out how he came to know Eckington 'vell', but he was gobsmacked. 'Even I'd never heard of bloody Eckington before I met Eric!' he said.

Abe had a great sense of humour and could turn any situation very quickly into a laugh. Normally there would be two or three from the North West on the bill every Saturday at Hanley and on the way back we would stop at a pub near Congleton called the Wagon and Horses, just making the last orders. This happened frequently and the landlord expected us, and let his customers know that wrestlers would be calling in and they could enjoy a chat and collect autographs. One night four of us called in – Colin Joynson, Steve Haggerty, Abe Ginsberg and myself. As we walked through the door, the landlord, with a sweep of his arm, announced, 'Here come the hard men!'

Abe, seizing the moment, hand on hip, minced his way to the bar and lisped, 'Four pink ginths, pleath landlord, and have one yourthelf.' The pub erupted into laughter!

Abe retired from wrestling in the late 1980s and ran a very successful antiques business in Macclesfield in Cheshire. He also featured in a weekly radio programme from Manchester advising and answering listeners' questions about antiques. He died suddenly in November 2001 and many wrestlers attended his funeral including myself, Vic and Bert Royal, and Colin Joynson. We had all travelled together to be there.

The service was held in a lovely village church and Abe's wife, Pauline, raised everyone's spirits when she remarked in her speech that, although it was unusual for a wife to speak, it was the only time in their long marriage that she had had the last word; and everyone laughed. But the most poignant moment for me was that, as we all filed out of the church, the music of Eva Cassidy's 'Over the Rainbow' drifted down the aisle, and almost everyone was in tears.

The (Even More) Eccentrics

'Is that bloody snake here again?'
Various wrestlers

An excellent way of gaining experience in the wrestling games particularly in the North of England in the 1950s and 1960s was in the small halls and clubs. There were a number of independent promoters who would visit the gymnasiums and amateur wrestling competitions to discover any talented lad with flair and a good physique, or send scouts on the same mission. Many of the top wrestlers climbed the tree of fame by this method.

Jack Taylor was one of these early promoters, himself being an ex-British, Commonwealth and European Champion. He knew precisely what to look for and many of the top television wrestling stars owed their beginnings to him.

Jack is still heavily involved in promoting wrestling shows mainly in the North of England and also edits a bimonthly magazine called *The Wrestling World*. It is packed with the latest news and stories regarding present and past times. In the latest edition he recalls the evening he came to my rescue back in the early days. We were both wrestling at a venue in Birmingham and Jack was topping the bill. After I had showered and dressed, it was about 10 p.m. I threw my gear into the boot and jumped into the car – but it wouldn't start. I struggled for about half an hour, but nothing I tried worked.

Jack came out and saw me, and realising that there was no way it was going to start, dived into his boot and brought out a tow rope. Then, believe it or not, he towed me all the 120 miles to my home in Stockport, and then drove back to his home in Leicester.

On the top of that, the next day he was wrestling in Edinburgh, so he had that journey to make there and back, because the next evening he was wrestling in Cambridge. En route to

Cambridge a sports car overtook him, headlights flashing and horn blaring, followed by gunshots. As the car shot passed, Jack saw Cowboy Jack Cassidy leaning out of the window waving his revolvers in the air. Hans Streiger was at the wheel, on their way to the same venue as Jack – absolutely crazy.

Jack Taylor was a hard man in the ring, but outside it he was a real gentleman. In a later conversation he reminded me of a time we teamed as tag partners against two lads who wrestled as the Undertakers (not to be confused with the original Undertaker).

We were topping the bill at a Lew Phillips Spectacular at the Digbeth Hall in Birmingham. The hall was packed to the rafters, and our opponents were diabolical villains and two referees would have been challenged to watch every angle and cope with the skulduggery of those two. About eight minutes of kicking, gouging, knees and elbows from them, Jack succeeded with a brilliant pin fall which both of the Undertakers vigorously contested. Soon after the bell Jack tagged me and I took the full force of their frustration. Turning me to the blind side of the ref, Alf Kent, they rained foul kicks and blows upon me. Then one of them kicked my legs from underneath me and sat on my head. The other one dived over the ropes, landing full length on me and driving the breath out of my body. I have to admit that at this point I went berserk. I grabbed one of them, tied his arms around the top rope with my speciality armlock, and then I chased the other across the ring and tied him firm and fast on the other side of the ring.

I then stormed back to the dressing room leaving the ref to count them out. Jack tried in vain to release them. The ref also tried unsuccessfully, and the promoter, Lew Phillips, also failed.

Lew came to my dressing room and persuaded me to return to the ring and untie them. The crowd however, were shouting to me to leave them there but I released them so the other bouts could continue.

Apart from learning the skill of being able to fall properly and master the holds and throwing techniques, a few of these men brought to the ring entertainment of a completely different aspect. Someone who springs to mind was called the Sheik, who had the added attraction of being able to insert needles into himself. I do not mean sewing needles – these were a similar size to large hat pins, which they probably were!

The first thing he did when he entered the ring would be to take these long needles from his bag and proceed to insert one through his cheek and out the other side. Another passed through the skin on his neck and yet another through his hand or wrist – I cannot remember precisely. The amazing thing would be that he never seemed to draw blood. He would then invite mainly the ladies to withdraw them and occasionally one brave soul would, but I have seen some faint at the attempt. The Sheik (Mike Taylor) had learnt the art of self-hypnosis and mind control, and his claim was that he was immune to pain.

Occasionally we were tag partners and our opponents would test his pain threshold by overenthusiastically lifting him above their heads and body slamming him; he would bounce about a foot off the floor. But, jumping to his feet, he paraded around the ring to prove that he had felt no pain. He didn't need to – I had felt it for him!

Mike is still involved with needles: I believe he has a tattoo business in his home town of King's Lynn.

Lord Bertie Topham

What a character he was; sporting a black silk top hat, a flowing black cloak lined with red silk, white gloves and grey spats covering his wrestling boots. And he would make his way down to the ring carrying a cane with a silver knob. He was a tall man, about 6 ft 2 "; well built and bronzed and very popular with the women fans, and they would clap and cheer him.

Striding majestically down to the ring, disdainfully ignoring the enthusiastic applause he looked every inch the toff. His valet followed (not for him a common second), also dressed in pin-striped trousers, a tail coat, silver-grey waistcoat and white gloves. Topham would then stand back to allow his valet to inspect that the corner was clean, mopping up any wet patches left by the previous wrestler, and would spray the corner padding with disinfectant.

Once Topham had entered the ring the valet proceeded to

remove his master's cloak and hat, brushing off any specks of dust with a silver-backed brush, and, after meticulously folding the rest of the ensemble, he would carry it grandly back to the dressing room. Moments later he emerged carrying a silver tray, crystal decanter and drinking glass, a silver spittoon bowl and a gleaming white napkin.

This last he would tie around his lordship's neck and then pour a glass of water for him then, while Topham delicately rinsed his mouth, his valet would approach his opponent.

After politely requesting to examine his hands and finger nails, he would then raise his arms and spray his armpits with deodorant. This procedure was repeated at the end of every round. You can imagine the response this received from some of Topham's opponents. They would grab the valet's immaculate jacket collar with one hand and the silver-grey waistcoat with the other and throw him as far as they could over the top ropes. Clearly, he must have been very experienced for he never seemed to suffer any injury, but the atmosphere that was generated led up to some first-class entertainment.

Topham was a powerful and classy wrestler, but what a villain – he could rival Mick McManus in the dirty tricks department. I don't think he ever read the rule book.

I never left the dressing room to watch any bouts unless it was someone in my weight division whom I'd never seen previously and could possibly be matched against in the near future. However, the two exceptions I never tired of watching were Lord Bertie Topham and Nagasaki. I don't think they ever met in the ring, but that would have been a bout worth buying a ringside ticket for.

The Snake Man

If a thousand people were asked their opinion of snakes, I am sure 99 per cent would say they prefer them at arm's length, or better still, behind glass in a zoo.

This opinion certainly applied to most wrestlers and referees and brings me to another character of the ring – The Snake Man. He was of moderate size and build, and to illustrate the jungle theme he would wear leopardskin trunks.

Coiled around his arm he carried a huge boa constrictor into the ring and, before the bell rang, he would poke its head into the faces of his opponent and the referee. They hated it; we all hated it. I know it was not the snake's fault, but the poor creature took the blame.

He would bring it to the venues in an Aladdin-style basket with a lid and, leaving it in the middle of the dressing room floor, he would go to report his arrival to the promoter and chat to his fans. As the wrestlers arrived, they would spot the basket and giving it a good kick, would mutter, 'Is that bloody snake here again?'

You can imagine, by the time the Snake Man got back, the snake was not well pleased! As he lifted the lid, its head popped out hissing like mad, its tongue darting in and out. He had to stroke its head until it calmed down.

I remember one time one of the lads came in, saw the basket and gave it a customary kick. Unfortunately, the basket rolled over and out rolled the snake. Slithering across the floor, it parked itself in a corner of an old settee that lay against the back wall of the dressing room. We all sat motionless as if we had been hypnotised.

Count Bartelli, masked as usual, entered the room and, throwing his bag on the floor, said to me, 'I've had a terrible journey down through the fog, Al.'

Whether the mask restricted his vision or he just did not see it, he flopped down on the settee right next to the snake and his hand must have caught it. The next moment it reared up and so did Count Bartelli. He must have broken the record for the sitting high jump by a good 3 ft. He was livid. It was a good job the Snake Man was not in the dressing room at that moment. I think Bartelli would have wrapped the snake around his neck.

I am afraid the rest of the evening did not get any better. After the Snake man's usual jabbing of the snake's head into the referee's face, with a mixture of fear and anger the referee knocked it out of his hands and it slithered out of the ring, and under the ringside seats.

In one minute flat, there were only three people left in the hall, two wrestlers and a referee. Everyone else had vanished.

That was the last time I personally saw the Snake Man, but he'd certainly left a lasting impression.

The Continental connection

After the austerity and privations of the war years, the Continent attracted many British wrestlers, and, in stark contrast to their rather formal Continental counterparts, the Brits must have seemed like a breath of fresh air.

Their flamboyant gear and showmanship made them very popular with the Continental fans. Although very few of the Continental wrestlers visited Britain, four wrestlers who impressed me the most were Jean Ferre, Maurice Tillet (the Angel), Julien Morice and Quasimodo. Each one of them brought their own special skills and personality, and, although I have appeared on the same bills with all of them, I confess to knowing very little about them on a personal level.

In saying that, their individual styles and techniques created a lot of interest with the British wrestling audiences both in the halls and television, so I feel that I should mention them in this book.

Jean Ferre

Before Big Daddy and Giant Haystacks arrived on the wrestling scene, one of the biggest men to climb into the ring was Jean Ferre. As he weighed in at 25 st., and stood at 6 ft 10 ", it was little wonder that he was called 'Atlas' in his native France.

As a conscript in the French army he quickly made a name for himself winning the force's heavyweight wrestling championship and, when he turned professional in the late sixties, he was promptly signed up by the leading European promoters, including Dale Martin. I was on the same bill with him at the Royal Albert Hall in London. His opponent was Big Bruno Elrington, a huge bearded Londoner, himself weighing 21 st., and standing at 6 ft 5 ".

To emphasise Ferre's exceptional strength: when Bruno claimed him and applied a side head lock, Ferre planted his feet, (which incidentally, were like two coal barges) firmly on the canvas and lifted Bruno clean off the floor by just flexing his neck muscles! Bruno's favourite submission hold was a bear hug, and although he caught Ferre in the hold, because of the Frenchman's massive chest expansion, he easily resisted it and overturned Bruno, gaining the one fall needed to win.

I met Ferre in Dumfries on a Jack Atherton promotion. Jack had booked both of us into a small hotel close to the venue. On arrival I booked in and asked the manageress if Ferre had arrived, with the intention of introducing myself. She confirmed that he had and led me to his room, knocking lightly at the door then, as she opened it we saw that Ferre was fast asleep on the bed. When I say 'on the bed', part of him was hanging over the end. It was the standard size, 6 ft 6" but his feet, and I have already mentioned their size, were hanging over the end by about 9 in.!

'Och, the poor man,' she whispered in a soft Scottish accent, 'but he will have to manage, I haven't got a bigger bed.'

Following his British tour, Ferre went to Montréal and then the States and became the famous André the Giant.

Julien Morice

Although wrestling fans enjoy the rough and tumble, power and brute strength of the heavyweights, true connoisseurs appreciate the speed, agility and pure wrestling science of the lighter men. Julien Morice was such a perfectionist and, in my opinion, on a par with George Kidd, Alan Sargeant, Jim Breaks, Johnny Saint and Jack Taylor.

Born in Toulouse, France, he was the son of a medical doctor and university lecturer. Hoping to follow his father, after leaving his local college he went on to study medicine at the universities of Toulouse and Paris, passing his final examinations to qualify as a doctor. To help to pay for his studies, he joined a wrestling club and within three years he had won both the French and European lightweight championships, and he decided to concentrate his energies in the wrestling rings full-time.

A month after he had arrived in Britain in 1967, he received his call-up papers for the French Army, returning to the wrestling ring as soon as he was discharged. He travelled the world, winning many trophies and accolades, but confessed to finding victory in Britain elusive, admitting that our light men were among the world's best.

Maurice 'the Angel' Tillet

Maurice Tillet was a reputable rugby player who played for his native France, between 1926 and 1929. He was in the forward line of the French team that played England at Twickenham in 1927.

At the time he was a young, handsome picture of health and physical fitness. He joined the French navy and aspired to the rank of a petty officer in a submarine flotilla. He left the navy when a glandular disturbance changed his appearance so dramatically that he was cruelly described as 'the nearest approach to a prehistoric man'.

Despite his grotesque appearance, to the people who knew him he was the same gentle, caring man but, because of the taunts of ignorant and insensitive morons, he was determined to hide himself away from the world in general.

He signed on as a seaman on a tramp steamer carrying cargoes to Indochina. The ship docked at Singapore and, to pass the time, Tillet went to a wrestling show. Top of the bill was Karl Pojello, former light heavyweight champion of the world. When Pojello spotted Tillet at the ringside, he felt a surge of pity for the huge, misshapen man. He befriended him and they became inseparable. Pojello convinced Tillet that, rather than hide himself he should go out and meet people and overcome his fear of rejection.

Tillet had done a little Greco-Roman wrestling in his early naval days, so Pojello persuaded him to return to France where Pojello trained him for two years. Because of his appearance, the promoters billed him as 'the Angel', and he became a very skilled and strong wrestler, feared by all the top heavyweights all over the world.

On 4 September 1954 in Chicago, Karl Pojello died from cancer and four hours later, Maurice 'the Angel' was found dead from natural causes. The general opinion, however, was that the Angel had died of a broken heart.

Quasimodo

The very name rings a bell (I could not resist that!). Quasimodo was another Frenchman who turned a cruel quirk of nature into a triumph of success. Because of a spinal deformity that resulted in leaving him hunchbacked, he would play it to the full.

Leaving the dressing room, swinging a huge handbell that deafened the people sitting nearest the aisle, he made his way to the ring. Dressed like the character from the book by Victor Hugo, he wore a brown tunic that reached to his knees and was tied with a length of rope. His deformity was quite an asset to him in the ring for, when his opponent tried to press his shoulders for a fall, he would just rock up and down on his hump.

Needless to say his name prompted many jokes around the dressing rooms and one of them that did the rounds was about the bell tower at Notre Dame. Every hour, so the joke went, Quasi would heave the huge bell as far as he could, catching it with his chin as it swung back. This would attract a large crowd in the courtyard. One day, an American tourist bragged that he could ring the bell the same way. His friends dared him to have a go, so up he climbed to the bell tower. He took hold of the bell, swung it out as far as he could and caught it on his chin as it swung back. It lifted him clean over the tower parapet and he landed flat on his back in the courtyard.

As Quasi scrambled down the steps, a gendarme was standing over the American and asked, 'Do you know this man, Quasi?'

Quasi, bending over, looked at him and said, 'No, his face doesn't ring a bell.'

Another joke was that Esmerelda came home from shopping with a wok.

Quasi asked, 'Are you going to try Chinese cooking?'

'No,' she replied, I've bought it to iron your shirts on.'

All of this he took in good part, but the one that had me laughing all the way home in the car was Esmerelda meeting Quasi and saying, 'What is that bulge in your pocket, are you glad to see me?'

'No,' he replied 'It's a photograph of my dad.'

Colin Joynson wrestled him a couple of times in France, and I remember him telling me that it was like trying to wrestle a three-wheeled bike. Whichever way he tried to turn him, he just went the other way.

He wasn't a frequent visitor to Britain and soon disappeared from the scene. As he was a very quiet and sombre man, I don't think any of us got to know him.

Tag wrestling rules

1. There are two wrestlers in a team; only one man from each team is allowed in the ring at a time.
2. To change places, the man in the ring has to 'tag' or touch his partner.
3. The second man must wait for the 'tag' outside the ropes on the ring apron, and must retain hold of the length of cord attached to the corner post.
4. He may not climb into the ring until 'tagged' but may move along the apron as far as the tag-cord and his outstretched hand will permit.
5. Once the 'tag' is made, one partner is released and the second man takes over.
6. There is no limit to the number of switches a team can make.
7. Tag-team contests are usually scheduled for forty minutes' duration, or can be decided within that time if one team can gain a knockout, two pin falls or secure two submissions.
8. In all contests, the referee's decision is final in respect of falls or submissions gained or disqualification of any man or team.

Those were the rules, and nobody took a blind bit of notice of them. Very often it would finish up with all four wrestlers in a heap with the hapless referee underneath.

There were some diabolical strokes pulled on the blind side of the referee during any of these melees, and it was an unwritten law that you took your share of the bumps in tag wrestling. In the event of a big bump or receiving cuts and bruises, as in show business, you had to carry on. 'Press on regardless' was the motto.

I was tagging with my partner Judo Pete Roberts (The Judokas) and had only been in the ring for a couple of minutes when I claimed my opponent (no names) and hyped him over close to his corner. Catching him in a headlock, I put my hand down on the canvas to gain a little more leverage. His partner leant through the ropes and stamped on my hand. The pain shot up my arm and I realised I would not be able to break my fall with my right hand for the remainder of the bout, not knowing whether I had broken any bones or not. Pete however, did more than his share for the rest of the time in the ring and I managed to finish the bout.

The next morning I showed my hand to my wife. It was swollen and bruised and she thought it looked as though I had a splinter in the centre of my palm and she tried to remove it with tweezers.

I leapt about 6 ft in the air since the splinter was in fact a fragment of bone protruding through the skin and I was left with a hole in my hand. However, it was fifteen years before it began to trouble me and I had to have surgery to remove scar tissue.

The Masked Men

'If I could play like that, I would not be sitting here drinking a pint of beer with three other cauli-eared, plug-ugly wrestlers.'
Anon

The Outlaw, the Crusader, the Red Devil, the Red Scorpion, the White Phantoms tag team, Dr Death, Count Bartelli, the Zebra Kid, and the most famous of all, Kendo Nagasaki; these were the names on the lips of millions of fans during the decades of the 1960s, 1970s and 1980s.

Every Monday morning in shops, offices, hair salons and factories throughout the country, the Saturday afternoon wrestling was relived; every hold, throw and foul was dissected by the armchair experts. The masked men of wrestling thrilled and intrigued everyone. They were shrouded in mystery, for no one knew their identity unless they were beaten. Then, according to the rules, they had to unmask. Crowds would pack the halls in the hope that they would witness such an event, but it rarely happened.

Dr Death, an American wrestler, came to England during the early 1960s and instantly made a name for himself by beating some of our best heavyweights. But then, at the height of his popularity, he mysteriously disappeared from the British scene. He returned again in 1969 for three bouts against Steve Logan, Mick McManus and Mike Marino, after which he vanished again.

I know that wearing a mask was purely showmanship with most of the wrestlers, but in the case of Dr Death was it more personal than that? Could he have been a politician or a member of the Senate acting out his fantasies? We will never know.

Worthy of a mention, another regular visitor from America was George Bollas, better known as the Zebra Kid. Just under 6 ft in height, he weighed over 24 st., but in spite of his bulk he was remarkably fast on his feet. He wore an amazing mask of black and white stripes, exactly like a zebra. A black vest and trunks completed his outfit. He was very popular with the fans, but unfortunately his career abruptly ended following two eye operations in 1969.

Bartelli and Nagasaki

A bout between two masked men was virtually unknown because it was inevitable that one of them would lose and would have to unmask to reveal his identity. He could still wrestle on, but the mystique would have disappeared. However, one such bout did take place between Kendo Nagasaki and Count Bartelli. Both of them were so confident of winning that a fight was arranged at the Victoria Hall, Stoke-on-Trent.

Bartelli had fought for twenty-five years without ever being defeated and with a record of about 5,000 bouts which at that time had not been equalled in British wrestling – you can imagine the excitement of the fans as the battle of the giants commenced. Fighting was under American rules, with no rounds, no time limits and only one fall or submission required to win.

With blood seeping from under the mask of Bartelli, the contest ended in a knockout for ace judo man Nagasaki. Bartelli retired to the dressing room to have a head wound stitched, later returning to the ring unmasked and was revealed as millionaire Geoff Condliffe from Crewe, Cheshire. He continued to wrestle for a short while after, but devoted most of his time to running his huge garage business. He died in the early 1990s.

Kendo Nagasaki, at 6 ft 4 ", stood out from them all. He was a masked man with a difference; fans and wrestlers alike were baffled by this mysterious man whose identity was a closely guarded secret. I know from experience that he was an expert in the martial arts, including kendo, the art of Japanese sword fighting. He was a great wrestler but, as with most martial arts experts trained by the Japanese Samurai warriors, there is a fine line between expertise and brute force.

I remember sharing a dressing room with Kendo in Altrincham, Cheshire. As he unpacked his bag he discovered he had brought with him two left boots instead of a pair. I said I would see if I could borrow a pair for him from the other lads, but no one had feet as big as his, so he had to force his right foot into a left boot.

His opponent was a big wrestler called Bull Davies, and he did not get that name for nothing. At the first bell, when they claimed one another in the referee's hold, I noticed Bull Davies's shoulders shaking with laughter. He then turned quickly and threw Nagasaki over the top rope. The set of steps that led up to the ring apron were made of solid wood weighing over half a hundredweight; Nagasaki pressed them over his head and hurled them into the ring at Bull Davies. He ducked and the steps hit the middle rope on the far side of the ring and, luckily, catapulted back. If they had missed the rope and gone through, they could have very well killed someone sitting ringside.

Afterwards I asked Davies why he was laughing at the start of the bout and he told me, 'When we came together in the referee's hold, I looked down and there were these two huge black boots pointing in the same direction on the white canvas. It was the funniest sight I have ever seen!'

Mind you, he wasn't laughing at the end – he was decisively beaten!

A few weeks later, Nagasaki was matched against the Bolton heavyweight, Billy Howes. Now I have fought Howes and I can tell you that he was one of wrestling's hard men, rough, rugged and economical with the rules. He once drop kicked me clean over the top ropes and I landed on to the ringside seats that had been vacated about thirty seconds before by spectators who regularly experienced the occurrence.

But to return to the Nagasaki–Howes bout: apparently this was a needle match to settle some sort of altercation between them from a previous fight. Billy Howes had complained bitterly after losing that Nagasaki had used unfair tactics, namely, karate blows with his fist, on the blind side of the referee. This accusation seemed a bit rich, since Billy was no angel, believe me.

However, Billy had practised judo in his younger years and in the heat of the moment challenged, 'If you want to use judo, I will meet you any time,' or words to that effect.

At home with my trophies and memories.

*With Norman Wisdom and Johnny Briggs.
You can't help laughing when you're with Norman.*

With Princess Anne at the Save the Children Fund charity event. Johnny, with legs suitably broken, is out of the picture.

Top of the bill with 'Mr TV' himself, Jackie Pallo, at the King's Hall in Derby. Note that Brian Glover (Leon Arras) was also on the bill.

Photograph by Stewart Darby.

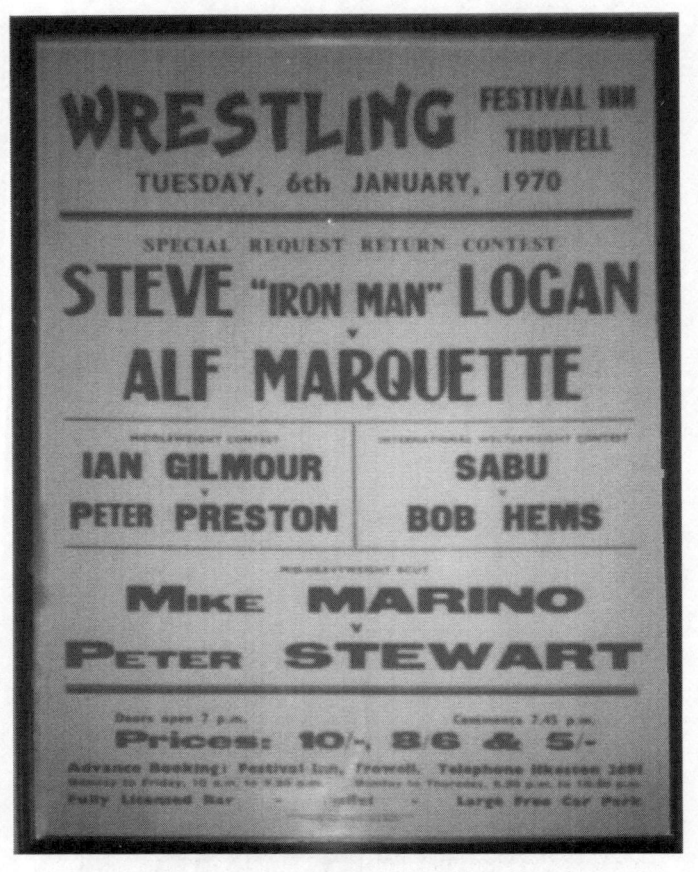

Topping the bill again, this time the Festival Inn in Trowell against the 'Iron Man'.

At a reunion with, from the left, Colin Joynson, Mick McManus and John Kenny.

Here I am with 'Cowboy' Jack Cassidy.

With former wrestler Hans Streiger.

With actor Duncan Preston.

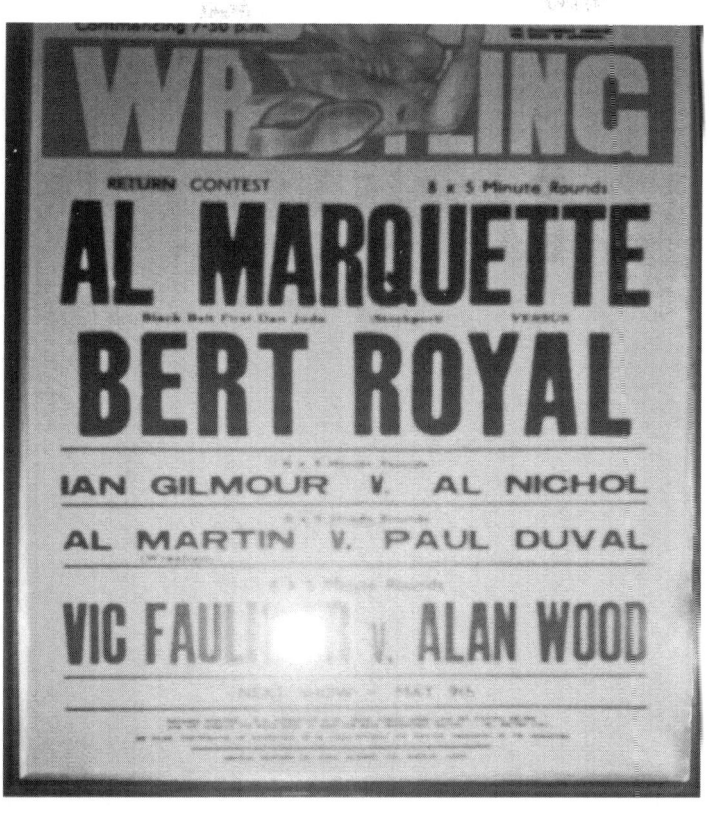

Top of the bill – again!
Bert Royal is the opponent this time in Bolton.

The last time I had a photo taken with my old mate Pat Roach before he was counted out for the final time.

Off on a golfing holiday with my old friend Johnny Briggs. He's not my son and I'm not his father.

This is an old one! I'm the one on the left with actors Tom Courtney and Julie Goodyear.

With actor Kevin Whately who, like Pat Roach, was part of the cast of the hugely successful Auf Wiedersehen, Pet.

With a host of celebreties, mainly from the cast of Emmerdale, *at a charity function.*

You never lose it!
Tony Barton will testify to that!

My celebrity golfing buddies: Johnny Briggs, David Beckett, who is the husband of my great friend Anne Kirkbride (Deirdre from Coronation Street*) and Geoff Hinsliff. Both David and Geoff had roles in 'The Street'.*

With Rick Wakeman and Patrick Mower.

Sharing a joke with former Yorkshire and England cricket captain Brian Close.

Singing with Sir Norman and Stan Boardman. You can't keep Norman out of the picture.

With former Everton football legend Duncan McKenzie.

From my days as a judo teacher at the 'Shin-Bu-Kan' (True Fighting House) in Stockport.

The wrestler's reunion in Kent.

This is me today – a sprightly eighty-one years of age.

The promotion was arranged to be held at the King's Hall, Belle Vue and I was to referee it. I had already been booked to fight at the Victoria Hall, Hanley, the same night but a substitute was arranged in my place.

It was a packed house at Belle Vue that evening, and as the time approached I made my way to the ring, passing Billy's cubicle on the way. I saw him sitting, waiting for his announcement. He was dressed in full judo kit (judogi), but as my eyes travelled down, he was wearing on his feet his wrestling boots!

I said to him, 'Billy, you can't wear boots! Apart from the fact that it's against the rules, you look a right bugger.'

'I don't care what I look like, Al,' he answered, 'there is no way I'm getting into that ring without my bloody boots. I don't know how you do it.'

I have officiated at many judo contests in my career, but never one like this one. Talk about fair play, etiquette, and the oriental love of protocol – they kicked the stuffing out of each other. My judo master, Kenshiro Abbe, must have been spinning in his grave. There was no time limit set; they had agreed to slog it out in the ring until one of them submitted. Trying to referee such a fracas was a nightmare. Nagasaki's manager would lean under the ropes to grab Billy's ankle, while Nagasaki chopped him in the throat. Billy would retaliate by jumping out of the ring and smacking the manager.

After about twenty minutes of conflict they both finished up outside the ring, scattering the crowd in all directions. I had no choice but to disqualify them both. The Belle Vue crowd loved every minute of it, but it was a night I would not have liked to repeat.

Nagasaki always entered the ring wearing the traditional kendo attire: a black skirt, breastplate, sword and the awesome mask. He would then perform the warrior's ritual of throwing salt around the ring to ward off evil spirits.

He never lost a bout and the fans, intrigued by his mysterious persona, would wait patiently outside the dressing room in the hope of spotting him leaving. They had noticed that half a little finger was missing on one hand and tried in vain to catch him out. He arrived and left every venue masked, and if anyone followed him he was a past master at shaking them off, travelling miles before removing the disguise.

We were billed together in Dundee and I arranged to meet him at an all-night petrol station just off the M6 near Preston. When we arrived back at about 2 a.m., he could not start his car. I wonder if the young chap serving in the kiosk remembers helping to push the car around the forecourt. He would have something to tell his children if he had known he was among the very few to have seen Nagasaki without his mask.

He was big, strong, very fit and an expert judoka and that was why the concealing mask was never in danger of being removed until during a televised bout in 1975 against Big Daddy who pinned him against a corner post and hauled off the mask to reveal his opponent's face.

Dressing room banter

When a dressing room is shared by a few wrestlers you have to be very careful what you are saying, as sometimes they can be as bad as women, and rumour spreads like wildfire. A juicy bit of gossip can do the rounds of all the venues, and if juicy enough can last for some time, much to the discomfort of the poor victim.

I have fallen victim myself a few times. On one occasion the incident involved my teenage daughter. As a martial arts exponent I wrestled in a white judogi jacket and pants, so consequently they had to be washed every time they were used. Hurriedly packing my bag I just grabbed my gear, and arriving at the dressing rooms, I prepared to get changed. Sadly in my haste a bra, belonging to my daughter Lesley, had become hooked on to my jacket in the airing cupboard and, yes you've guessed it. Out it fell on to the floor.

I remember Les Kellet falling about laughing and telling everyone, including Kent Walton, that the only reason I wore a judogi in the ring was to cover up my bra.

Those incidents took a lot of living down. Another time I was embarrassed was while I was travelling by boat to the Isle of Man. Before the ferries, the boats to the island were like small liners – very luxurious, with a dance floor and a grand organ playing all the popular dance tunes of the day.

I was sitting with three other wrestlers enjoying a drink, when I was approached by a lady who requested me to play 'Red Sails in the Sunset'. Completely taken by surprise, I replied, 'I beg your pardon?'

'Aren't you the organist?' she said. He was taking a well-earned rest at that moment.

'Madam,' I answered her, 'if I could play like that, I would not be sitting here drinking a pint of beer with three other cauli-eared, plug-ugly wrestlers.'

There followed what can only be described as a deafening silence until one of the lads piped up: 'Bloody hell Al, when you wrestle at Blackpool Tower, do you stand in for Reg Dixon as well?'

Mentioning Blackpool Tower, the first time I wrestled there, being unfamiliar with the layout, I asked the doorman to direct me to the dressing rooms. He pointed to the rear of the building and as I walked around the corner I was relieved to see Mick McMichael, the Doncaster wrestler who wrestled for the Scottish team, casually leaning against a door.

Mick was a born prankster and always on the lookout for a leg pull. With hindsight I should have known better than to ask him the way to the dressing rooms.

'Down those stairs,' he pointed to a set of stairs. 'It's not very well lit, but keep going. There's a door at the end of the passage – the dressing rooms are through there.'

Slowly I began to make my way down, I could just about make out a strip of light from under the door at the end of the passage. The smell down there should have alerted me. I had taken about ten paces when I heard an almighty roar, followed by snarling and a clawing at the bars on either side of me. Not knowing whether to go backwards or forwards, I decided to head for the strip of light from under that door. I realised that there were cages on either side of me, and I imagined paws raking through the bars ready to tear me to pieces.

The roars had now become a crescendo of ear-splitting noise, and I turned sideways on to present myself as a thinner target. With my blood frozen in my veins, and my heart trying valiantly to pump it around my body, and almost feeling the breath of those animals on my neck, I made a final lunge for the door. The instinct for sheer survival had the sweat pouring out of me and, as I opened the door, there sat Mick, grinning all over his face.

Mick McMichael was at that moment the most hated man in my life – the bugger who had sent me through the place that housed all the wild animals from the circus. Lions, tigers – you name them, I had met them. I thought he had been a little abrupt when I had asked him the way, now I realised that he had been trying to stop himself from laughing.

The irony of it was that he had been standing in front of the dressing room door in the first place. I forgave him, eventually.

Very early in Bert Royal's career, while he was still a teenager, he was on one occasion booked to wrestle at a venue in Carstairs, Scotland. Not being used to travelling such a distance alone he teamed up with three seasoned North of England wrestlers.

It was a long, tiring and slow journey, and, after their bouts they arrived back at Carstairs railway station just in time for the eleven thirty train. Exhausted Bert sunk back into his seat, and feeling drowsy he asked the other lads to wake him when he had arrived at Wigan station, Lancashire, should he fall asleep, which he promptly did.

The next thing he knew was being shaken awake and being told he had reached Wigan station. Groggily he grabbed his bag and shouting his thanks he jumped on to the platform. The guard blew his whistle and the train chugged away. Rubbing the sleep out of his eyes, Bert looked up and read the name of the station, 'Lockerbie' – only ten minutes from Carstairs, and over a hundred miles from Wigan.

Bert did not see the funny side and to this day, he still doesn't. He spent a very uncomfortable night, and caught the first train back the following morning. I don't know if Bert was ever matched against any of those lads in later years, but if he was, I bet they rued the day.

I was wrestling Colin Joynson at the Southport Floral Hall. The bout was being televised and in the fourth round he aimed me into the ropes and as I bounced off he hit me in the face with a forearm smash which flattened my nose, spraying blood down my judo jacket.

Arriving home later that night I ran a bath half full of cold water and placed my jacket and trousers carefully in to soak out the blood. I was awakened by a loud shriek and rushing to the bathroom found my wife Betty gazing in horror at what appeared to be a body covered in blood, floating in the water. The air was blue and she had no sympathy at all for my swollen nose.

Another story that did the rounds of the dressing rooms was that the London wrestlers, Peter Rann and MC Sammy King, were driving back from an engagement one night when Peter, feeling peckish, spotted a fish and chip shop. This was when sixpence (old money) would buy a very large bag of chips.

Asking Sammy if he wanted anything, Sammy handed Peter a five pound note.

'Just chips,' he answered, making no attempt to go for them.

Now Sammy was well known for letting everyone else do the fetching and carrying for him, so Peter replied, 'With pleasure Sammy.'

Arriving back at the car he plonked this huge bag of chips on Sammy's knees. He had bought him five pounds worth! Sammy's face was a picture of disbelief.

But one story that kept us all laughing, and as a matter of fact still does for me until this day, was about the promoter Jack Atherton and his colleague Billy Hargreaves.

Jack was the typical northern bloke with no edge to him at all. In spite of how much money he may have had, he chose to live in the same terrace house that he had always lived in. He would ring me saying, 'Al, can thee pop round for thee list of venues for next month?' Entering his lounge-cum-office, a huge table dominated the centre of the room, the top of it piled high with posters, programmes and all the paraphernalia involved with wrestling. Undaunted he would delve into the pile and pull out the correct piece of paper; he alone knew where everything was.

Whenever wrestling was on at the Dumfries Drill Hall, Jack and Billy would deliver the wrestling ring in a battered old van and, after erecting it, they would toddle off to the local cinema.

On this particular afternoon the film being shown was *Bonnie and Clyde*.

On leaving the cinema they were surprised to see two policemen prowling around their van and writing down the number plate. The policemen knew them, because they were often on duty at the Drill Hall, but had decided to have a leg pull at their expense. Approaching their van, Jack and Billy were taken aback when they were asked to produce their licence and to account for where they had been and where they were going.

'Come off it lads,' said Jack, 'tha' knows me and Billy.'

Unperturbed, the policeman carried on.

'We've been informed a van resembling this one has been involved in a bank hold-up.'

Billy blurted out, 'We've been all afternoon in yon picture 'ouse,' jerking his thumb towards the cinema.

'Oh,' replied the cop, rocking on his heels, 'And what did you see then?'

Caught on the hop Jack blustered, '*McVitie and Price*.'

'*Bonnie and Clyde*, you daft bugger,' muttered Billy.

Wrestling for Charity

'Right, you've given us a football lesson in the first half... we'll give you a lesson in wrestling if you don't ease up.'
Bobo Matu

In 1967, the *Manchester Evening News* sponsored a charity wrestling bill at the Free Trade Hall in Manchester, in aid of the News-vendors Benevolent Institution (Old Ben). It had been organised by the *TV Times* area sales manager, Fred Markey. Fred and I had first met through our daughters' mutual interest in horses and he had arranged a charity gymkhana – both our daughters, Lesley and Julie, were competing.

He explained to me that each year the management team of the *TV Times* took it in turn to organise various charity events. I suggested to him that as all-in wrestling was viewed by millions of people every week on television, a good money-spinner would be a charity wrestling programme. He enthusiastically agreed and so I introduced him to a local promoter.

The programme read:

Count Bartelli	v	Dennis Mitchell
British Empire Heavyweight Champion		
Judo Al Marquette (Stockport)	v	Jack La Rue (Australia)
Peter Linberg (Manchester)	v	Karl von Krama (Germany)
Tag Match		
The Pye Brothers Dominic and Casey	v	Pat Curry (USA) Colin Murphy (Ireland)

How Fred managed to persuade him to present a bill that would have done justice to venues such as Belle Vue or even the Royal Albert Hall, I shall never know. It was a stroke of genius on Fred's part and the event was a complete sell-out.

The hall was crammed to the doors with fans anticipating an evening packed with action and thrills; they were not disappointed as the clash of the Titans commenced. Most of them had never seen Bartelli without his mask and the ladies must have been pleasantly surprised to find out that he was quite a handsome man.

Although I was in the dressing room I could hear the crowd shouting and cheering as Bartelli made his enormous strength count, pinning Mitchell for the winning fall in the fifth round.

I was next into the ring against Jack La Rue. It does not matter how many years you have been wrestling or how many bouts you may have had, you always got a twitch of nerves when you are facing an opponent you have never seen before and know absolutely nothing about.

La Rue was about the same height as me but I was giving away about 2 st. in weight. In the opening round, as I was a practising judoka, when we met in his centre of the ring I made my customary bow. As I bent forward he shot out his foot and kicked me in the chest. It caught me off balance and down I went. I came to my feet and he mockingly bowed to me so I kicked him back and he went flying. This brought the house down and we had both marked our cards.

At one point during the match the belt of my jacket came loose and La Rue grabbed it, wrapped it around my neck and threw me across the ring. As I came to my feet he lunged at me again, but I tripped him and he landed flat on his face. I applied a back hammer lock with my foot instead of the orthodox hand hold. With my foot pinning him to the canvas, I casually retied my belt around my waist and the crowd went crackers.

I won the bout with a hand tie and sleeper hold and I was very proud to be presented with the *Manchester Evening News* Challenge Trophy for the most exciting bout of the evening.

The fans enjoyed the mixture of wrestling skills and dexterity exhibited by Pete Linberg and Karl von Krama. Linberg demonstrated his awesome strength by easily pressing Krama to arm's length over his head and body slamming him to the canvas. As he staggered to his feet Linberg caught him in his bone-crunching bear hug, winning the bout with a submission in the sixth round.

In contrast, the rule bending and sometimes vicious wrestling of the Pye Brothers kept the crowd on the edge of their seats. Dominic was the team captain and after about twenty minutes into the bout, I think he realised that there was no way he and Casey could out-wrestle Curry and Murphy so they resorted to pulling every dirty trick in the book. This cut no ice with the referee, Paul Carpantier, and he disqualified them both.

That ended a very satisfying and rewarding evening for the fans and Old Ben didn't do too badly either.

As with most areas around the country, hospitals, schools and many other worthy causes would very often approach the television wrestlers to open garden fetes, judge competitions and beauty contests, present prizes and cheques, and form darts teams to play against the pubs. I captained the wrestlers' football team for a few years and mainly we played the Showbiz Eleven captained by Richard Beckinsale. The fun we had and indeed the crowds that turned up also enjoyed the outrageous stunts that were pulled on the pitch.

The girls from the cast of *Coronation Street* were always willing to kick off for us – Pat Phoenix, Julie Goodyear, Diana Davies and Jennifer Moss. Jennifer Moss not only volunteered to kick off, she also played for a while and I remember one time she asked the referee to send her off for foul play, so that she could have a bath before the game ended. We all got wind of this and started fouling each other so the referee sent us all off. You can imagine Jennifer's face when we all trooped in; she could not get out of the bath quick enough!

Because of our commitments, Sunday was the only day that we could all guarantee to turn up and the response from the public was brilliant. Even on cold, miserable, wet days the crowds would be there.

We raised thousands of pounds for hospitals and cancer research and, just to illustrate the support, at one hospital in Stockport called Offerton House, the pitch was situated behind the hospital about two miles from the town centre. The match had to be delayed for over an hour because of the huge crowd and the queue of cars blocking the roads. Of course I had overlooked the need to inform the police and they were not very pleased with me; so a smacked wrist and 'don't do it again' for me!

One occasion we were playing a team of professional footballers led by Alan Ball senior and including Tommy Pye, Stuart Pearson, Paul Reaney, Bill Foulkes, Matt Woods and more illustrious names. All they did was to just stand there and pass the ball around and then wallop – the ball was in the back of the net! We were all running around like headless chickens. The score at half time was about 31–0; all very satisfying for the footballers but not very watchable for the spectators.

In the dressing room we were all sharing, Bobo Matu said to them, 'Right, you've given us a football lesson in the first half.' They all laughed and Bobo went on, 'We'll give you a lesson in wrestling if you don't ease up.'

I think the final score was about 32 all, and I am sure everyone enjoyed the fun.

Offerton House Hospital provided residential care for patients of all ages, particularly those affected with Down's Syndrome. Anyone who has had the experience of knowing or working with them will all say what delightful and affectionate people they are.

The general manager, Ernest Bosanko, told me how much the patients young or old enjoyed to watch the wrestling on television on a Saturday afternoon. So I approached one of the Manchester promoters, Jack Atherton, and asked him if there was a possibility of accommodating some patients at one of his promotions within a distance of thirty miles, and perhaps at a discount price. Jack agreed, and Mr Bosanko would arrange for a small coach to take them to the venue.

After the bouts the wrestlers would meet with them and pose for photographs. The carers told us that it was the highlight of their week, and they were forever asking when their next trip would be. On other occasions the staff would accompany some patients on shopping expeditions, and it was on one such trip that my first wife, Betty, and I happened to be shopping in the precinct.

We were looking at an outside display of flowers when I was spotted by a crocodile of about a dozen youngsters. Breaking away from their carers, they rushed over to me and flinging their arms around me caught me off balance. Betty was holding on to me, but I'm afraid that both of us went headfirst into the display, knocking the vases all over the place. The shop owner rushed out to see what had happened, not at all happy too see his stock trampled on. However, when I explained the circumstances he was very understanding and refused to accept payment for the ruined flowers.

It was not my day that Saturday. As we left the precinct we stopped at a store and bought a television set, arranging to collect it later in the afternoon. I had parked my car outside the shop ready to load the TV set and, as I came out, there was a woman traffic warden putting a parking ticket on my windscreen. I explained to her that I was just collecting a television set, but with her expression frozen on her face, remarked, 'You're parked on double yellow lines.' Then, looking closely at me she said, 'You're Al Marquette aren't you? My son is a fan of yours. We saw you at Belle Vue last week, could I trouble you for your autograph please?'

I replied that if she gave me his name and address I would be happy to give him a signed photograph, which I did as soon as I arrived home, thinking that possibly I may be let off the booking. But sadly no, a few days later I received notification of my offence and instructions to pay the fine.

Some of the most dangerous matches were played against the ladies. Sister Grace from the Stockport Infirmary rang to ask me if we would play a team of nurses from the Stepping Hill Hospital, also in Stockport. I agreed, but what she failed to tell me was that four of those 'nurses' she had recruited were actually players from Stockport County FC, dressed in nurse's uniform complete with wigs and make up. If any wrestler fell, and the nurses made sure we did by kicking our ankles and tripping us up, we were put into splints and carted off on a stretcher to be dumped behind the goal posts. It didn't make for good football but it was a great laugh and the crowd enjoyed it too.

Pat Phoenix owned a country pub at Buxworth, near Chinley

in Derbyshire, with a football field adjoining and she would often ring me to organise matches against her regulars for her favourite charities. Pat always looked a million dollars and she was a perfect hostess with plenty of food and drink laid on for the lads. She was a good sport and always joining in the fun, but her husband, Alan Browning, rather than play football, would stand on the sidelines strumming a banjo and taking the mickey. Once he arrived wearing an immaculate cream suit and as he strummed away on his banjo, four of us picked him up and dunked him in the mud puddle in the middle of the pitch. He was shocked, but he took it in good part – I think!

The last time I met Pat, we had both been invited to judge the Miss Derbyshire Rose beauty competition along with Alan Browning and the managing director of the Ferodo Brake Lining Company and his wife, at Chapel-en-le-Frith near Buxton, Derbyshire. It was a very difficult decision since all the contestants were beautiful and it was very close, but choose we had to.

The great advantage of being involved in a sport at professional level, whether it be wrestling, boxing, football, cricket, rugby or any other sport, is that the friendships and camaraderie continue, even after retirement.

In the early 1980s I took up golf and joined Northenden Golf Club, where I met some of my dearest friends. Because of my wife's longstanding illness, I liked to play very early in the morning, about 6.30 a.m. in order to be home to care for her; and it was on the first tee about twenty years ago that I first met Johnny Briggs.

He was playing early because he had to be back at Granada Studios for rehearsals. We played eighteen holes together and found we had much in common. I had met a lot of stars of *Coronation Street* in the early days and Johnny was a good friend of Spencer Churchill, the ex-Mr Universe and professional heavyweight wrestler. Apparently they trained together at the same gym in London. We have been great pals ever since, travelling to golf tournaments all over the country, holidaying in Florida, and playing a round of golf at the club, whenever possible. It was Johnny who introduced me to David Beckett and we hit it off at once.

David is an actor who appeared in *Coronation Street* for fourteen months as the handyman boyfriend of Deirdre (Anne Kirkbride). He has also had parts in TV shows such as *The Bill*, *Emmerdale* and *Heartbeat*, plus numerous adverts, and he has performed in many stage productions. I was invited to their wedding when he and Anne were married. When I lost my wife, Betty, they invited me to their home many times, and I was very moved by their kindness and support.

Two other people that I have met and become good friends with are Geoff Hinsliff and his wife, Judy. They too opened up their home to me after my sad loss, offering any help that I should need. Geoff, as you must know, played Don Brennan in 'The Street' for many years and has also had a long career in TV and stage productions.

Another of The Street's characters – and what a character – that I have met is Bruce Jones (Les Battersby). Bruce has told me that, as a boy, I was his hero. He had lived with his grandmother in Manchester and she would take him along with his school mates to Belle Vue to watch wrestling. He has told me that his grandmother could not afford the judo kit that his friends all had when they practised my holds and moves in the street, so she cut a pair of pyjamas down for him. What can I say to that!

When I married my present wife, Pat, in 1999, David was my best man and Anne was Pat's Matron of Honour. Geoff and Judy were our guests of honour. It was a very quiet ceremony with just the family and friends present. The weather was super and it was day that you remember for ever.

It was at that time that Anne, or 'Deirdre', was sent to jail and Anne tells of how she was amazed at the number of letters she received from well-wishers, including lawyers offering their services and prison officers advising her how to keep her 'nose clean'! Pat baked her a cake with a file inside. Crazy times!

Pat and I both have a daughter each and my daughter, Lesley, always tells the story of the time when she was about ten years old, and I had decided it was time to teach her to defend herself. We arrived at my club, the Shin-Bu-Kan, and the first thing she saw as she entered the room was a big notice on the wall which read: 'PLEASE DO NOT BLEED ON THE MAT!' That put her off right away, but she did become proficient in self-defence. Lesley does not have children but Pat's daughter, Ellie, has two – Charlotte, who is eighteen, and Alex, who is fifteen and a keen football fan. So I have inherited a granddaughter and a grandson, and we are all one big happy family.

Finally, I must mention the other great pals at the golf club – Ray Hall, Cliff Brown, Stewart Redwood, Roger Metcalfe, Jimmy Nutter, Brian Branagh, Gerry McMenamin, Father Danny Canning, Dennis Brown, Jim Garrin, Tom Cunningham, Dennis Dawson, Geoff Noor, Joe Kavanagh and Captain Tony Parkinson. None of whom may be in show business, but they are a real bunch of comedians and bandits!

I joked recently to someone that I'd never clocked anyone at the club – yet! Then I remembered one incident from a time shortly after I'd joined Northenden. I was stood outside with a chap who I happened to know and was arriving to be interviewed for membership. In the car park, there was a lad aged about eighteen, trying all the car doors. This chap asked him what he was doing.

'What's it got to do with you?' this lad shouted back. 'F—k off!'

The chap he was saying this to was quite a big fellow and it surprised me, but I didn't say anything because I was fairly new to the club and didn't want to cause a scene. Anyway, this lad continue trying doors and the chap shouted to stop or he'd call the police.

'Send who you f—king well like!' he retorted, then walked up the steps to the club and tried the door I'd just come out of, which had a security buzzer on it. He started back on the cars again and the chap said he'd had enough of this and started towards the lad. I told him to leave it to me. I walked over to this lad and put my face in his.

'Now,' I began, pointing to my friend, 'he's a gentleman, I'm not. You tell me to f—k off once and I'll smash your face in.'

He looked a bit taken aback and turned to walk away across the green.

'Hey!' I shouted. 'Up there!' I pointed to the drive.

'But I don't live that way,' he replied.

'I don't care where you live, up there!' And he waltzed over to the drive and we never saw him again. Old habits die hard!

During the summer months, Geoff, Johnny, David, and I, play on the Celebrity Golf Circuit organized by Paul Gaskell Promotions. We play along with top stars, past and present from the soaps, theatre, sports players from football, cricket, rugby darts and snooker champions, musicians, singers and comedians. Names that seem to have gone on for ever, many hosting events such as the Sir Norman Wisdom Classic and the Stan Boardman Classic to name two, and my apologies to whom I have not mentioned, since there are so many who are happy to give their time and talents for such worthy causes.

Causes such as, children's hospices, scanner appeals, hospitals, powered wheelchairs and other equipment that adds to the quality of life for physically challenged children and adults. However, without the sponsorship and generosity of the British and overseas companies, none of this would happen. Great prizes are donated, exotic holidays, television sets, computers and sports equipment, and occasionally, a car, for any one who is lucky enough to score a hole in one. I have never seen this achieved, maybe someone, someday will strike it lucky.

At the end of the day's play, we return to our rooms to prepare for the evening, an excellent dinner, during which each celebrity is introduced by Paul and invited to stand.

As you rise everyone applauds and you acknowledge him with a wave. Pat Partridge, the famous referee never fails to raise a laugh where upon his introduction, instead of applause he is booed by all the celebrities. Fishing into his top pocket out comes the red card and with his familiar gesture we are all ordered 'off'.

After the meal, Willy Thorne or Dennis Taylor auction off all the memorabilia donated and signed by the sporting personalities such as shirts, footballs, snooker cues, cricket bats, golf clubs and posters, the proceeds going into the pot. Over £300,000 was raised in 2003 to help mainly children's charities and proceeds have always averaged a similar amount since then.

A cabaret then follows to bring the evening to close. Comedians such as Dickie Day, Norman Collier, Stan Boardman and his son Paul, Johnny More, Mickey Gunn, Max Peters, Tony

Barton and last but not least by any means, Steve Womack.

Then, reviving their past hits, vocalists appear like the Bachelors, John Miles, Pattie Gold and her husband and musical director Steve, Rick Wakeman, Kit Rathbone, Berni Flint, Shel McCrae – the lead singer with the Fortunes, the multitalented Brendon Healy and the brilliant pianist and comedian 'Fingers' Colin Henry, Sir Norman Wisdom who, although in his eighties, can still sing his song 'Don't Laugh at Me' with all the emotion and pathos that made it such a massive hit for him as a younger man.

Still the list goes on: the Haughton Weavers, Pete Conway, who has the distinction of being the father of Robbie Williams as well as being an accomplished vocalist in his own right, Clive Jones of the Black Abbots and Colin and Leslie Gibson, all giving their time freely to make the evening an outstanding success for benefit of charities dedicated to the lives of children and others in need.

Sadly, Paul Gaskell died of a heart attack in March 2004. He is very sadly missed by all the celebrities, sponsors and children's charities he and his wife Christine worked so hard for. However, his very good friends Alan and Gill Clark have taken over the tour and are doing an excellent job. The charities will continue to receive the same financial help and I know I speak for all those who participate when I say Alan and Gill will receive the same support that was given to Paul and Christine.

Usually the hotel is part of the golf course complex, but sometimes it can be situated three or four miles away. On one occasion Johnny Briggs and I had travelled down together to a course near Shrewsbury. Usually an overnight stay is arranged for us but we both had engagements the following day, so we needed to drive back after the cabaret finished.

We were leaving about midnight when Geoff Hinsliff asked for a lift back to the hotel, rather than wait for the transport, the distance being about three miles. However, none of us knew the area, and away from the well-lit roads we soon found ourselves lost. After a while, and many mutterings of 'I think it's down that way,' or 'For God's sake, where the hell are we?', we came to a small humpbacked bridge. To our relief, a man was walking towards us. Johnny wound down his window and asked directions to the hotel.

The chap thought about it for a minute then, looking at Johnny, he said, 'I know you, don't I?'

Johnny replied, 'Please, do you know the way to such a hotel?'

The man scratched his head and said, 'Yes, keep on this road for about half a mile. I do know you, don't I?'

'Probably,' replied Johnny, 'so we keep on this road for half a mile, and then which direction?'

'Oh yes,' the man went on, 'about half a mile from here you turn right at the lights. I'm sure I know your face.'

Johnny turned to me and said, 'For God's sake, drive on, Al,' but at that moment a police car pulled up behind me.

A policeman and woman approached our car and the policeman said, 'This bridge is not a sensible place to park on, especially at midnight, what is your problem?' The policewoman was grinning all over her face and nudging her colleague. Clearly she had clocked Geoff and Johnny. I told them we were asking the directions to Geoff's hotel. I explained we were dropping him off before continuing to pick up the motorway to Manchester.

'Follow us,' the officer commanded. I had the awful feeling that we were about to be taken to the police station for breathalysing, but in fact he led us to the door of the hotel, waited for Geoff to go inside, and then instructed me to follow him again. He escorted us to the motorway, and with a cheery wave from them both we were on the way home – aren't our police wonderful!

Another amusing incident happened at an event organized by Unigate Foods with the proceeds going to the Save the Children Charity. Johnny Briggs, David Beckett, Geoff Hinsliff and I had been invited to a golf day, to be followed with an introduction to the Princess Royal, Patron of the Fund, who would be accepting a cheque to the value of £500,000.

After the meal, instead of lining up to meet her, we all stood around in groups until she was brought to meet us. Johnny and I were standing together when the Princess came over. She was utterly charming and we chatted about wrestling and golf.

The Princess confided that her grandmother, the late Queen Mother, was a keen wrestling fan and would watch it on television on a Saturday afternoon. Also, that her husband Commander Tim Laurence enjoyed a game of golf. Turning to Johnny, she inquired how he had become involved with the charity.

Johnny replied, 'Ma'am, I had to agree or Al would have broken both my legs!'

At this remark she threw her head back and laughed out loud. Afterwards everyone was asking me what we had said that had made her laugh so much. Jokingly I told them that she had asked for my room number, but I had turned her down.

The Reunion

I recall travelling down to Kent on a lovely summer's day in August 2003, along with two other well-remembered pals of mine, Steve Haggerty and Gypsy John Kenny. We were on our way to a reunion, to be met there by Colin Joynson and his wife Helen, and Johnny Saint. They had travelled down the day before, breaking their journey.

The reunion of the television wrestlers from the sixties, seventies and eighties, is arranged annually by Tony Scarlo and Joe D'Orazio, and hosted by one of the top heavyweights of his days, Wayne Bridges and his charming wife Sarah. Pat Roach was the other organiser, before his untimely death in 2004.

There were a few wheelchairs and crutches, plenty of cauliflower ears and broken noses, but I don't think any one of us regretted our time in the ring. As a matter of fact, if a promoter started a senior tour, they would be queuing up to climb through the ropes again. There were far too many famous faces present to name them all, but a few stood out as still looking extremely fit – Mick McManus, Pat Roach, Spencer Churchill, Jack Taylor, Johnny Kincaid, Brian Maxine, Danny Flynn, Cowboy Jack Cassidy, Joe Cornelius, Leon Fortuna, Steve Grey, Klondyke Jake, Roy Plunkett, Peter Szakacs, Tiger Joe Robinson, Steve Veidor, Doug James, Joe Cusak and Paul Duval.

All had packed the halls all over Britain and Europe in their heyday. Bitter rivals, who wouldn't pass the time of day with one another – but all that was forgotten as they sat together enjoying a drink or two, sharing their memories.

I was disappointed that Billy Two Rivers couldn't make it. I would have liked to have chatted with him about the past experiences we had shared. Unfortunately Bert Royal and Vic Faulkner had to cancel due to a family illness.

Talking to my old rival, Mick McManus, I asked why Jackie Pallo had not arrived. Mick said that he had rung Jackie to invite him and Jackie had replied, 'No Mick, I won't be coming, I've got a bad back and my hip is playing me up, so I will give it a miss.'

Then he asked, 'Will Ray Hunter be there?'

'I don't think so,' said Mick.

'He died a little while ago.'

'Oh,' came the reply, 'well if he does turn up, give him my regards.'

I think Jackie must have been feeling the bumps!

There were lots of stories being bandied about, some unprintable – but some were really funny, like this one that Gypsy John Kenny told me:

Apparently he was travelling back from a venue in London with three other wrestlers, Pedro the Gypsy, Gorilla Reg Rae, and Catweasel. Driving them in his sleeper van was the referee, Emile Polvy. The three wrestlers were asleep in the van when it was stopped by a police road block. It appeared there had been an armed robbery in the area and the police, on high alert, were stopping all vehicles passing through.

It was a filthy night, the rain coming down like stair rods, and clearly the two policemen were peed off at having to leave the comfort of the patrol car. Approaching the van cautiously one of them asked Emile the reason for his journey, and Emile answered that he and his three other passengers were returning from London. With suspicion written all over his face, one of them opened the van door and asked them all to get out. A quick search revealed nothing.

Turning to one of them he asked, 'What's your name?'

'Gypsy John Kenny,' he answered.

Turning to Pedro he asked the same question.

'Pedro the Gypsy.' The policeman eyed him, his impatience beginning to show.

'And yours?' He looked at Reg, then rocking on his heels he gave his companion a look enough to say, 'Any more of this and we'll run them in'.

He almost spluttered when the answer came, 'Gorilla Reg Rae!'

'Are you trying to make a monkey out of me?' he said, not realising at first what he had said.

The other lads had to turn away to stop themselves from laughing.

Facing Catweasel he muttered, 'And I suppose you are bloody Tarzan?' Even he had to smile at his own witty remark.

'No, I'm Catweasel,' came the answer.

Glaring into Catweasel's eyes and with his face red with suppressed anger he went on, 'Right, for the last time, before I run all of you in, give me your real name.'

For a brief moment there was silence, then Catweasel spoke, 'Gary Cooper.' That was the final straw, the lads burst into laughter and even the other policeman was beginning to see the funny side.

Eyeball to eyeball the first one then demanded, 'You can prove that can you?'

Catweasel produced his driving licence, everything was confirmed, and they were allowed to continue their journey, laughing all the way.

To return to the reunion, I must mention the fans. It never ceases to amaze me how, after all these years, they turn out in their hundreds to meet their old heroes, packing into Wayne's country inn, lining the roads just for a chat and an autographed photograph.

One fan, Terry Parker, writes to me reminding me of bouts and opponents down the years, bringing back wonderful memories. Terry and his pal, Roy Plunkett, probably know more about wrestling than any of us.

At the end of the afternoon, a minute's silence is held and a long list of wrestlers who have passed on is read out. The 2003 list ran: 'Giant Haystacks, Big Daddy, Abe Ginsberg, Les Kellet, Steve Logan, Eric Cutler, Lord Bertie Topham and the commentator Kent Walton.'

Then, after many handshakes and goodbyes, it's the long drive home and we look forward to the following year.

The Best of Times

'I think we'll have a drop of claret, Jack.'
Bert Assirati

Two questions that most wrestlers will recognise, and indeed have been asked are: first, is it fixed? and second, did we make any money?

A lot of rubbish has been said about wrestlers and wrestling. A number of times people have told me that their dad was in the same class at school as Billy Two Rivers or even Nagasaki! Also they contend that we, the wrestlers, arrive early at the venues so we can rehearse the moves – absolute rubbish!

At the start of every month, each of us would receive a contract from our respective promoter through the post, informing us of venues, times and dates. Opponents were not mentioned and it was not until you actually saw the advertising posters that you were aware whom you were matched with. Admittedly there was a great deal of showmanship, but that is what made professional wrestling so popular.

The promoters knew exactly how to arrange bouts to maximise ticket sales but, at the same time, ensuring the fans were buying their money's worth of excitement. Heroes were matched with villains and the passions those bouts aroused brought avid fans back to the halls and television sets, week after week after week. Grannies would lose all sense of propriety as they hurled insults at the villains, the referee and even the TV screen, and even today young people can still remember their grannies ranting and raving and throwing cushions at the set as Mick McManus and Jackie Pallo strutted around the ring after flattening Granny's favourite hero.

If I had a pound for every time some clever clogs had said to me, 'The body slams, suplexes, arm and leg locks must be fixed, otherwise you could get seriously hurt', I would be a millionaire How you would fix a body slam is beyond me. You are picked up by your opponent, lifted as high as he can manage, and then slammed down on to a very hard ring floor, and he could not care less whether you were hurt or not. It is up to you to break your fall properly and if you don't, tough luck. Breaking a leg or an arm signifies that you need to get back in the gym and learn your job

The same applies to the leg and arm locks. If you don't know how to turn so that the pressure is not against the joints, of course you are going to get hurt. It's as simple as that.

Admittedly we would sell it. We would stagger around feigning injury and playing up to some of the wrestler's specialities. As I have said on several occasions, that was what the fans loved to see. But most of the techniques are genuine holds and throws, practised by wrestlers from all over the world. Testimony to this are the many wrestlers from my era who are now practically crippled with arthritis and other complaints, due to years of body slams and the rest.

Wrestling in my bare feet, I have to admit, wasn't without risks either, especially when you were thrown out of the ring and landed on the ringside seats. Apart from getting them stamped on many times by my opponents, I've had the skin taken off my toes as I've skidded along the rough canvas floor and, though this is all part of the game, on one occasion it turned out to be very nasty indeed.

I was wrestling Honey Boy Zimba at the Wryton Stadium in Bolton. Honey Boy was a popular lad and the crowd was certainly enjoying the clash. Having been a bodybuilder, he was extremely strong and stood six-foot tall and the bout was fast and furious. At one point, he picked me up and threw me out of the ring. I skidded along the floor, scraping the skin off the side of my big toe on my left foot. Climbing back in the ring, my Second slapped a plaster over my toe and I never gave it a second thought.

However, two days later, I was sat at home and my knee began to swell. It soon got so bad I had to call a doctor out. He arrived, took one look and ordered an ambulance to rush me to hospital. I was x-rayed on arrival where blood poisoning was diagnosed. Had it been left longer, God knows what might have happened but, with a few weeks' rest and recuperation, I was able to return to the ring. The doctor later showed me the x-ray of my foot and pointed out a small white line across every toe.

'Did you know every toe had been broken?' he asked.

I shook my head. 'No,' I said, 'I had no idea.'

'That figures,' said the doctor. 'Where there's no sense, there's no feeling.'

I used to laugh at the many cartoons in the papers and magazines depicting two wrestlers in the ring, one being caught in a painful-looking leg hold while saying to his opponent, 'How's the wife these days?' It always reminds me of Les Kellet – he always talked to you in the ring. He would hype you over, hold your hand down on the canvas and say, 'Mind your little hand,' and then stamp on it. Or he would say, 'Mind your little head,' and then knee drop on to it; and he was always very polite when he threw you over the top rope – he would bid you, 'Ta ta!'

I remember Jack Atherton once telling me he was wrestling Bert Assirati at Belle Vue, Manchester. Bert had him in a side head lock and whispered to him, 'I think we'll have a drop of claret, Jack,' smashing him on the nose, breaking it – 'claret' flowing all over the canvas.

Yes, they did talk in the ring, but not to ask how the wife is. Believe me.

I recall enjoying a cup of coffee in a snack bar at a Midlands venue some years ago, shortly before I was due to drive home. A distinguished-looking man approached me and explained his eighteen-year-old son was an avid wrestling fan whose ambition was to become a TV wrestler. Whom should he contact, he enquired.

I asked how proficient his son was as an amateur wrestler and how long he'd been training for. Also, how many competitions had he won at local or national level. He replied that his son was yet to wrestle in any form but was a 'strong lad'! I then asked if he had any experience in the martial arts – judo, karate, or Aikido. 'No,' he replied, 'but he's very acrobatic.'

Did we make any money? A pal of mine retired from wrestling with £100,000 in the bank which he put down to dedication, never refusing a bout, seldom losing, and the fact that his uncle had died and left him £98,000!

Seriously, though, if you compare pro rata with today's salaries, yes, you could earn a good living. I was earning about £100 a week and, compared to today's money, I and many other wrestlers had a good standard of living. You could earn more from the big venues such as the Royal Albert Hall or televised bouts but, though there were competitions with prize funds, I could never enter them because my judo skills weren't allowed. Jackie Pallo, Kendo Nagasaki, Giant Haystacks and Big Daddy were the big earners from the old days because they were on television such a lot. Professional wrestling is a hard, rough, bruising and often dangerous sport, but I would not have missed one single minute of it for anything.

I've been asked if I ever watched myself on the TV when I took part in televised bouts – I did when I could, but we didn't have video recorders in those days so invariably I'd be travelling to an even while the highlights were televised, but I managed to catch about four or five of my appearances and, even if I say so myself, I quite enjoyed it! I have nothing to watch and reminisce, unfortunately, because the programmes were in big film cans and not on videotape and my search for old footage has proved fruitless. I believe they show the old bouts in Canada and Australia where they have proved to be very popular. In fact, if anyone does have any old footage from my days, I'd love to hear from you.

I reckon I had about 3,000 bouts during my wrestling career and lost fewer than twenty, which isn't a bad record. The injuries I suffered included a broken jaw, broken nose, broken ankle, broken toes, broken fingers, broken rib, lost my front teeth, and gained a cauliflower ear. Call them the spoils of war but I still fell fighting fit with no real after-effects from all the knocks I've had down the years.

I put it down to looking after myself and keeping things in moderation and exercising every day. I do tension exercises based on a Charles Atlas routine I learned years ago – no weights – just pushing against your own body strength. I've never over-eaten and avoid foods that, if taken in excess, can prove detrimental, and have never put any weight on. I still get asked if I teach or grade judo, but it's not something I wish to do any more. I've lost touch with the sport, but I could certainly coach someone up to black belt standard if I wanted to. I still reckon I could hold my own if I had to! I'd advise any youngster to take up a physical sport and judo is perfect, rather than just sit in front of the TV all day long playing video games. If they don't, they will regret it later in life – I guarantee it. I don't take a pill of any description and I put it down to my past and my fitness levels.

So, to conclude, how do you bring to an end such a flow of great memories – put a lid on it, so to speak? Shall I pour myself a drink? Yes, and raise my glass and say to all the great names that I have mentioned in this book, and all the great names that I have not – *cheers*!

To the early years, when wrestlers made long, cold, foggy and frozen journeys so as not to disappoint their fans – *cheers*!

Finally, to the fans themselves who have supported their favourites down the years, and still continue to do so, sending us snippets of information they think will be of interest to us – *cheers*!

To all who have cheered us, jeered us and clocked us with their handbags, for the living experience, the drama and the wonderful world of wrestling, I raise a glass to each and every one of you – *cheers*!

Keep fighting.

Al Marquette

Photograph by Stewart Darby.

Photograph by Stewart Darby.

Photographs by Stewart Darby.

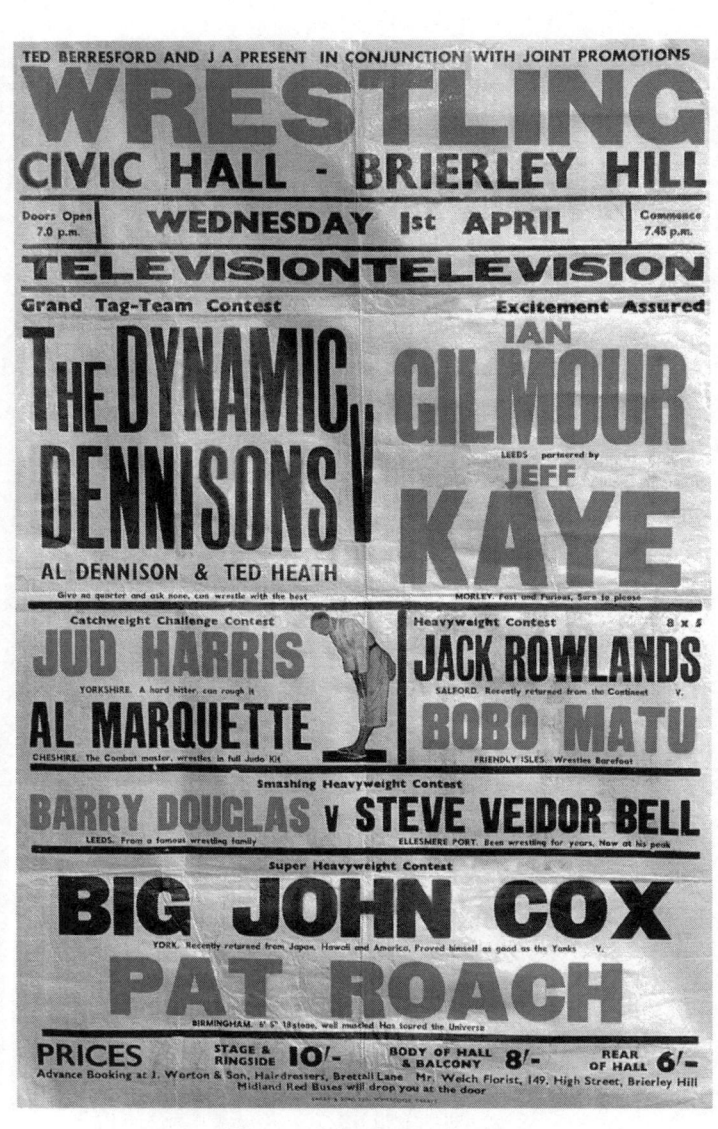

Photograph by Stewart Darby.